SIDE *by* SIDES

PRESTWICK HOUSE, INC

ROMEO AND JULIET

WILLIAM SHAKESPEARE

Shakespeare's text

on the left;

a modern rendering

on the right.

Prestwick House

P.O. Box 658 • Clayton, DE 19938
Tel: 1.800.932.4593
Web site: www.prestwickhouse.com

ISBN-13: 978-1-58049-517-2

Copyright ©2004 by Prestwick House, Inc.

Table of Contents

DRAMATIS PERSONAE

Chorus.
Escalus, Prince of Verona.
Paris, a young nobleman, kinsman to the Prince.
Montague, head of one house, at odds with Capulets.
Capulet, head of one house, at odds with Montagues.
An old Man, of the Capulet family.
Romeo, son to Montague.
Tybalt, nephew to Lady Capulet.
Mercutio, kinsman to the Prince and friend to Romeo.
Benvolio, nephew to Montague, and friend to Romeo
Tybalt, nephew to Lady Capulet.
Friar Laurence, a Franciscan.
Friar John, a Franciscan.
Balthasar, servant to Romeo.
Abram, servant to Montague.
Sampson, servant to Capulet.
Gregory, servant to Capulet.
Peter, servant to Juliet's Nurse.
An Apothecary.
Three Musicians.
An Officer.
Lady Montague, wife to Montague.
Lady Capulet, wife to Capulet.
Juliet, daughter to Capulet.
Nurse to Juliet.
Citizens of Verona; Gentlemen and Gentlewomen of both houses;
Maskers, Torchbearers, Pages, Guards, Watchmen, Servants, and
Attendants.

PROLOGUE

[Enter Chorus.]

CHOR: Two households, both alike in dignity,
    In fair Verona, where we lay our scene,
    From ancient grudge break to new mutiny,
    Where civil blood makes civil hands unclean.
5   From forth the fatal loins of these two foes
    A pair of star-cross'd lovers take their life;
    Whose misadventur'd piteous overthrows
    Doth, with their death, bury their parents' strife.
    The fearful passage of their death-mark'd love,
10   And the continuance of their parents' rage,
    Which, but their children's end, naught could remove,
    Is now the two hours' traffic of our stage;
    The which if you with patient ears attend,
    What here shall miss, our toil shall strive to mend.

[Exit.]

PROLOGUE

[Enter Chorus]

CHOR: *Our story is set in the city of Verona, where two equal and respected families hold an old grudge which now breeds a new clash, promoting civil unrest and much woe for all citizens. The feud engulfs the two sides, and only the deaths of two star-crossed lovers will bury the parents' hatred. The fateful end to their love, their deaths, and the continuous clash of their parents' rage will be the story presented on our stage during the next two hours. Please be patient with our efforts, for we will try to fix any errors we commit.*

[Exit.]

ACT I

SCENE I

Verona. A public place.

[Enter Sampson and Gregory with swords and bucklers of the house of Capulet.]

SAMP: Gregory, on my word, we'll not carry coals.

GREG: No, for then we should be colliers.

SAMP: I mean, an we be in choler, we'll draw.

GREG: Ay, while you live, draw your neck out of the collar.

5 SAMP: I strike quickly, being moved.

GREG: But thou art not quickly moved to strike.

SAMP: A dog of the house of Montague moves me.

GREG: To move is to stir, and to be valiant is to stand.
Therefore, if thou art moved, thou runn'st away.

10 SAMP: A dog of that house shall move me to stand. I will take the
wall of any man or maid of Montague's.

GREG: That shows thee a weak slave; for the weakest goes to the wall.

SAMP: 'Tis true; and therefore women, being the weaker vessels, are
ever thrust to the wall. Therefore I will push Montague's men from
15 the wall and thrust his maids to the wall.

ACT I

SCENE I
Verona. A public place.

[Enter Sampson and Gregory (with swords and bucklers) of the house of Capulet.]

SAMP: *Gregory, really, we'll not put up with insults.*

GREG: *No, for then we should be mere servants.*

SAMP: *I mean it; and if we be angry, we'll draw our swords.*

GREG: *Yes, but while you are alive, escape the Prince's noose.*

SAMP: *Being upset, I will strike quickly.*

GREG: *But you are not quickly moved to strike.*

SAMP: *A dog of the house of Montague moves me to anger.*

GREG: *To move is to stir, and to be valiant is to stand firm. Therefore, if you are moved at all, you will run away.*

SAMP: *A dog of that house could cause me to stand. I will take the inside position to any man or maid of Montague's.*

GREG: *That shows you to be a weak slave, for the weakest goes to the wall.*

SAMP: *It's true; and therefore women, being the weaker vessels, are ever thrust to the wall. Therefore, I will push Montague's men from the wall and thrust his maids to the wall.*

GREG: The quarrel is between our masters and us their men.

SAMP: 'Tis all one. I will show myself a tyrant. When I have fought with the men, I will be civil with the maids; I will cut off their heads.

GREG: The heads of the maids?

20 SAMP: Ay, the heads of the maids, or their maidenheads. Take it in what sense thou wilt.

GREG: They must take it in sense that feel it.

SAMP: Me they shall feel while I am able to stand; and 'tis known, I am a pretty piece of flesh.

25 GREG: 'Tis well thou art not fish; if thou hadst, thou hadst been poor John. Draw thy tool! Here comes two of the house of Montagues.

[Enter two other Servingmen, Abram and Balthasar.]

SAMP: My naked weapon is out. Quarrel! I will back thee.

GREG: How? turn thy back and run?

SAMP: Fear me not.

30 GREG: No, marry. I fear thee!

SAMP: Let us take the law of our sides; let them begin.

GREG: I will frown as I pass by, and let them take it as they list.

SAMP: Nay, as they dare. I will bite my thumb at them; which is a disgrace to them, if they bear it.

35 ABR: Do you bite your thumb at us, sir?

SAMP: I do bite my thumb, sir.

ABR: Do you bite your thumb at us, sir?

GREG: *The quarrel is between our masters and us, their men.*

SAMP: *It's all the same. I will show myself a tyrant. When I have fought with the men, I will be polite with the maids—I will cut off their heads.*

GREG: *The heads of the maids?*

SAMP: *Ay, the heads of the maids, or their maidenheads. Take it in whatever sense you would.*

GREG: *They must take it in the sense that they feel it.*

SAMP: *They shall feel me while I am able to perform, and it is known that I am a pretty piece of flesh.*

GREG: *It is well that you are not fishy; if you were, you would have been a cheap meal. Draw your weapon! Here come two of the house of Montague.*

[Enter two other Servingmen, Abram and Balthasar.]

SAMP: *My sword is out of its holder. Quarrel! I will back you.*

GREG: *What? Turn your back and run?*

SAMP: *Don't worry about me.*

GREG: *No, indeed. I do fear you!*

SAMP: *Let us keep the law on our sides; let them begin.*

GREG: *I will frown as I pass by, and let them take it as they like.*

SAMP: *No, as they dare. I will insult them, which is a disgrace to them if they take it.*

ABR: *Do you bite your thumb at us, sir?*

SAMP: *I do bite my thumb, sir.*

ABR: *Do you bite your thumb at us, sir?*

SAMP: *[Aside to Gregory.]* Is the law of our side, if I say ay?

GREG: *[Aside to Sampson.]* No.

40 SAMP: No, sir, I do not bite my thumb at you, sir; but I bite my thumb,
sir.

GREG: Do you quarrel, sir?

ABR: Quarrel, sir? No, sir.

SAMP: But if you do, sir, I am for you. I serve as good a man as you.

45 ABR: No better.

SAMP: Well, sir.

[Enter Benvolio.]

GREG: *[Aside to Sampson.]* Say 'better.' Here comes one of my master's
kinsmen.

SAMP: Yes, better, sir.

50 ABR: You lie.

SAMP: Draw, if you be men. Gregory, remember thy swashing blow.
[They fight.]

BEN: Part, fools! *[Beats down their swords.]*
Put up your swords. You know not what you do.

[Enter Tybalt.]

TYB: What, art thou drawn among these heartless hinds?
55   Turn thee, Benvolio! look upon thy death.

BEN: I do but keep the peace. Put up thy sword,
Or manage it to part these men with me.

SAMP: [Aside to Gregory.] *Is the law on our side if I say yes?*

GREG: [Aside to Sampson.] No.

SAMP: No, sir, I do not bite my thumb at you, sir; but I do bite my thumb, sir.

GREG: Do you quarrel, sir?

ABR: Quarrel, sir? No, sir.

SAMP: But if you do, sir, I am ready for you. I serve as good a man as you.

ABR: No better.

SAMP: What's your point, sir?

[Enter Benvolio.]

GREG: [Aside to Sampson.] Say "better." Here comes one of my master's kinsmen.

SAMP: Yes, better, sir.

ABR: You lie.

SAMP: Draw swords, if you are men. Gregory, remember your slashing blows.
[They fight.]

BEN: Part, fools! [Beats down their swords.] Put up your swords. You do not know what you do.

[Enter Tybalt.]

TYB: What, have you drawn against these cowards? Turn, Benvolio! Look upon your death.

BEN: I only keep the peace. Put up your sword, or help me part these men.

15

TYB: What, drawn, and talk of peace? I hate the word
    As I hate hell, all Montagues, and thee.
60   Have at thee, coward!   *[They fight.]*

*[Enter an officer, followers of both houses, and three or four Citizens
with clubs or partisans.]*

CITIZENS: Clubs, bills, and partisans! Strike! beat them down! Down
    with the Capulets! Down with the Montagues!

[Enter Old Capulet in his gown, and his Wife.]

CAP: What noise is this? Give me my long sword, ho!

WIFE: A crutch, a crutch! Why call you for a sword?

65 CAP: My sword, I say! Old Montague is come
    And flourishes his blade in spite of me.

[Enter Old Montague and his Wife.]

MON: Thou villain Capulet!—Hold me not, let me go.

M. WIFE: Thou shalt not stir one foot to seek a foe.

[Enter Prince Escalus, with his Train.]

PRINCE: Rebellious subjects, enemies to peace,
70   Profaners of this neighbour-stained steel—
    Will they not hear? What, ho! you men, you beasts,
    That quench the fire of your pernicious rage
    With purple fountains issuing from your veins!
    On pain of torture, from those bloody hands
75   Throw your mistempered weapons to the ground
    And hear the sentence of your moved Prince.
    Three civil brawls, bred of an airy word
    By thee, old Capulet, and Montague,
    Have thrice disturb'd the quiet of our streets
80   And made Verona's ancient citizens
    Cast by their grave beseeming ornaments

16

TYB: *What, your sword is drawn, and you talk of peace? I hate the word as I hate hell, all Montagues, and you. Here I come, coward!* [They fight.]

[Enter an officer, followers of both Houses, and three or four citizens with clubs.]

CITIZENS: *At them, men! Strike! Beat them down!*
   Down with the Capulets! Down with the Montagues!

[Enter Old Capulet, in his gown, and his wife.]

CAP: *What noise is this? Give me my long sword, quickly!*

WIFE. *A crutch, a crutch! Why do you call for a sword?*

CAP: *My sword, I say! Old Montague has come and draws his blade to spite me.*

[Enter Old Montague and his wife.]

MON: *You villain, Capulet! Don't hold me; let me go.*

M. WIFE: *You shall not stir one foot to seek an enemy.*

[Enter Prince Escalus with his followers.]

PRINCE: *Rebellious subjects, enemies to peace, killers of your neighbors—will they not hear? What! You men, you beasts, who quench the fire of your evil rage with purple fountains issuing from your veins! On pain of torture, from those bloody hands throw your angry weapons to the ground and hear the sentence of your angry Prince.*

Three civil brawls, begun from angry words by you, old Capulet, and by Montague, have three times disturbed the quiet of our streets and made Verona's ancient citizens cast away staffs and pick up old weapons in order to separate your cancerous hate.

17

To wield old partisans, in hands as old,
Canker'd with peace, to part your canker'd hate.
If ever you disturb our streets again,
85 Your lives shall pay the forfeit of the peace.
For this time all the rest depart away.
You, Capulet, shall go along with me;
And, Montague, come you this afternoon,
To know our farther pleasure in this case,
90 To old Freetown, our common judgment place.
Once more, on pain of death, all men depart.
[Exeunt all but Montague, his Wife, and Benvolio.]

MON: Who set this ancient quarrel new abroach?
Speak, nephew, were you by when it began?

BEN: Here were the servants of your adversary
95 And yours, close fighting ere I did approach.
I drew to part them. In the instant came
The fiery Tybalt, with his sword prepar'd;
Which, as he breath'd defiance to my ears,
He swung about his head and cut the winds,
100 Who, nothing hurt withal, hiss'd him in scorn.
While we were interchanging thrusts and blows,
Came more and more, and fought on part and part,
Till the Prince came, who parted either part.

M. WIFE: O, where is Romeo? Saw you him to-day?
105 Right glad I am he was not at this fray.

BEN: Madam, an hour before the worshipp'd sun
Peer'd forth the golden window of the East,
A troubled mind drave me to walk abroad;
Where, underneath the grove of sycamore
110 That westward rooteth from the city's side,
So early walking did I see your son.
Towards him I made; but he was ware of me
And stole into the covert of the wood.
I, measuring his affections by my own,
115 Which then most sought where most might not be found,
Being one too many by my weary self—

If ever you disturb our streets again, your lives shall pay for the forfeit of
the peace. At this time, all the rest depart. You, Capulet, shall go along with
me; and, Montague, you come this afternoon to Capulet's castle, my common
judgment place, to know my further pleasure in this case. Once more, on pain
of death, all men depart.

[Exit all but Montague, his wife, and Benvolio.]

MON: Who started this ancient quarrel again? Speak, nephew; were you the
cause of it?

BEN: The servants of your adversary and yours were fighting before I did
approach. I drew my sword to part them. In that instant, came the fiery
Tybalt, with his sword drawn. He breathed defiance to my ears; he swung
his sword about his head and cut the winds. Nothing was hurt as the wind
hissed. While we were exchanging thrusts and blows, others came who fought
on each side, until the Prince came and parted us.

M. WIFE: Oh, where is Romeo? Did you see him today? I am glad he was not
at this fight.

BEN: Madam, an hour before sunrise, a troubled mind drove me to walk abroad
where, underneath the grove of sycamore trees on the west side of the city, I
did see your son walking. I went towards him, but he was aware of me and
stole into the cover of the woods. I, measuring his actions by my own, also
sought a place to be alone, being one too many by my weary self. I followed
my own mood and did not follow him. I gladly left the one who gladly fled
from me.

Pursu'd my humour, not pursuing his,
And gladly shunn'd who gladly fled from me.

120 MON: Many a morning hath he there been seen,
With tears augmenting the fresh morning's dew,
Adding to clouds more clouds with his deep sighs;
But all so soon as the all-cheering sun
Should in the farthest East begin to draw
The shady curtains from Aurora's bed,
125 Away from light steals home my heavy son
And private in his chamber pens himself,
Shuts up his windows, locks fair daylight out
And makes himself an artificial night.
Black and portentous must this humour prove
130 Unless good counsel may the cause remove.

BEN: My noble uncle, do you know the cause?

MON: I neither know it nor can learn of him .

BEN: Have you importun'd him by any means?

MON: Both by myself and many other friends;
135 But he, his own affections' counsellor,
Is to himself—I will not say how true—
But to himself so secret and so close,
So far from sounding and discovery,
As is the bud bit with an envious worm
140 Ere he can spread his sweet leaves to the air
Or dedicate his beauty to the sun.
Could we but learn from whence his sorrows grow,
We would as willingly give cure as know.

[Enter Romeo.]

BEN: See, where he comes. So please you, step aside,
145 I'll know his grievance, or be much denied.

MON: Many a morning has he been seen there, with tears adding to the fresh morning's dew, adding more clouds to the clouds with his deep sighs. But as soon as the cheering sun should in the farthest east begin to raise the shady curtains from Aurora's bed, away from this light my sad son steals home and in his chamber pens himself up, shuts up his windows, locks fair daylight away, and makes himself an artificial night. Black and forbidding must this mood be unless some good counsel can remove its cause.

BEN: My noble uncle, do you know the cause?

MON: I neither know it, nor can I learn about it from him.

BEN: Have you asked him about it?

MON: I have asked him, both by myself and many other friends; but he is his own heart's counselor, and he keeps to himself. He is so secretive and is so far from understanding as the bud is, which is bit by an envious worm before the bud can flower and spread its sweet leaves to the air or its delicate beauty to the sun. If we could learn the cause of his sorrows, we would willingly give a cure.

[Enter Romeo.]

BEN: Look, here he comes. Please step aside; I'll know the cause of his sadness or be denied only after much effort.

21

MON: I would thou wert so happy by thy stay
     To hear true shrift. Come, madam, let's away,
                    [Exeunt Montague and Wife.]

BEN: Good morrow, cousin.

ROM: Is the day so young?

150   BEN: But new struck nine.

ROM: Ay me! sad hours seem long.
     Was that my father that went hence so fast?

BEN: It was. What sadness lengthens Romeo's hours?

ROM: Not having that, which, having, makes them short.

155   BEN: In love?

ROM: Out—

BEN: Of love?

ROM: Out of her favour, where I am in love.

BEN: Alas that love, so gentle in his view,
160   Should be so tyrannous and rough in proof!

ROM: Alas that love, whose view is muffled still,
     Should without eyes see pathways to his will!
     Where shall we dine? O me! What fray was here?
     Yet tell me not, for I have heard it all.
165   Here's much to do with hate, but more with love.
     Why then, O brawling love! O loving hate!
     O any thing, of nothing first created!
     O heavy lightness! serious vanity!
     Misshapen chaos of well-seeming forms!
170   Feather of lead, bright smoke, cold fire, sick health!
     Still-waking sleep, that is not what it is!
     This love feel I, that feel no love in this.
     Dost thou not laugh?

22

MON: I hope that you do hear his true confession. Come, madam, let's leave.

[Exit Montague and wife.]

BEN: Good morning, cousin.

ROM: Is it so early?

BEN: It has just struck nine.

ROM: Ah, me! Sad hours seem long. Was that my father who left here so fast?

BEN: It was. What sadness lengthens Romeo's hours?

ROM: Not having that, which when you have it, makes the hours short.

BEN: In love?

ROM: Out—

BEN: Of love?

ROM: I am in love but out of her favor.

BEN: Alas, that love which is so gentle in its appearance should be so tyrannical and rough in reality!

ROM: Alas, that love, blindfolded as it is, should, without eyes, ever find pathways to his will! Where shall we dine? Oh, my! What fight was here? Yet don't tell me, for I have heard it all before. It has much to do with hate, but more with love. Why then, Oh, brawling love! Oh, loving hate! Oh, anything of nothing first created! Oh, heavy lightness! Serious vanity! Misshapen chaos from well-seeming forms! Feather of lead, bright smoke, cold fire, sick health! Still-waking sleep that is not sleep at all. This love that I feel that gets no love in return. Do you laugh?

BEN: No, coz, I rather weep.

175   ROM: Good heart, at what?

BEN: At thy good heart's oppression.

ROM: Why, such is love's transgression.
    Griefs of mine own lie heavy in my breast,
    Which thou wilt propagate, to have it prest
180   With more of thine. This love that thou hast shown
    Doth add more grief to too much of mine own.
    Love is a smoke rais'd with the fume of sighs;
    Being purg'd, a fire sparkling in lovers' eyes;
    Being vex'd, a sea nourish'd with lovers' tears.
185   What is it else? A madness most discreet,
    A choking gall, and a preserving sweet.
    Farewell, my coz.

BEN: Soft! I will go along.
    An if you leave me so, you do me wrong.

190   ROM: Tut! I have lost myself; I am not here:
    This is not Romeo, he's some otherwhere.

BEN: Tell me in sadness, who is that you love?

ROM: What, shall I groan and tell thee?

BEN: Groan? Why, no;
195   But sadly tell me who.

ROM: Bid a sick man in sadness make his will.
    Ah, word ill urg'd to one that is so ill!
    In sadness, cousin, I do love a woman.

BEN: I aim'd so near when I suppos'd you lov'd.

200   ROM: A right good markman! And she's fair I love.

BEN: A right fair mark, fair coz, is soonest hit.

BEN: No, cousin, I rather weep.

ROM: Good cousin, at what?

BEN: At the heaviness of your good heart.

ROM: Why, such is love's nature. Griefs of my own already lie heavy in my chest. This love that you have shown adds more grief to too much of my own. Love is a smoke that is raised by the perfume of sighs; when love is cleansed, it is a fire sparkling in the eyes of lovers; when it is crossed, it is a sea nourished with lovers' tears. What else is it? It is a most delicate madness, a deadly drink, and a healthy medicine. Farewell, my cousin.

BEN: Wait! I will go along with you. And if you leave me, you do me wrong.

ROM: Whew! I have lost myself; I am not here. This is not Romeo; he's somewhere else.

BEN: Tell me in earnest—who is it that you love?

ROM: What, shall I moan and tell you?

BEN: Moan? Why, no; but sadly tell me who.

ROM: You ask a sick man to make his will in sadness. These words are ill-timed to one that is so ill! In sadness, cousin, I do love a woman.

BEN: I aimed at that when I supposed you loved someone.

ROM: You are a good marksman! And the one I love is fair.

BEN: A pretty mark, fair cousin, is the soonest hit.

Rom: Well, in that hit you miss. She'll not be hit
     With Cupid's arrow. She hath Dian's wit,
     And, in strong proof of chastity well arm'd,
205   From Love's weak childish bow she lives unharm'd.
     She will not stay the siege of loving terms,
     Nor bide th' encounter of assailing eyes,
     Nor ope her lap to saint-seducing gold.
     O, she's rich in beauty; only poor
210   That, when she dies, with beauty dies her store.

Ben: Then she hath sworn that she will still live chaste?

Rom: She hath, and in that sparing makes huge waste;
     For beauty, starv'd with her severity,
     Cuts beauty off from all posterity.
215   She is too fair, too wise, wisely too fair,
     To merit bliss by making me despair.
     She hath forsworn to love, and in that vow
     Do I live dead that live to tell it now.

Ben: Be rul'd by me: forget to think of her.

220 Rom: O, teach me how I should forget to think!

Ben: By giving liberty unto thine eyes.
     Examine other beauties.

Rom: 'Tis the way
     To call hers, exquisite, in question more.
225   These happy masks that kiss fair ladies' brows,
     Being black puts us in mind they hide the fair.
     He that is strucken blind cannot forget
     The precious treasure of his eyesight lost.
     Show me a mistress that is passing fair,
230   What doth her beauty serve but as a note
     Where I may read who pass'd that passing fair?
     Farewell. Thou canst not teach me to forget.

Ben: I'll pay that doctrine, or else die in debt.   [Exeunt.]

ROM: Well, with that shot, you miss. She'll not be hit with Cupid's arrow. She has Diana's wisdom; and she is certainly most pure, for she never has been wounded by Cupid's weak childish bow. Nor will she be won by loving talk, nor the making of seductive eyes, nor will she open her lap, not even for enough gold to seduce a saint. Oh, she's rich in beauty. It is only sad that when she dies, her wealth of beauty will also die.

BEN: Then has she sworn that she will live a virgin?

ROM: She has, and in that virginity, she makes such a huge waste; for beauty, starved by her chastity, eliminates any chance of beautiful children. She is too fair, too wise, and wisely too fair; she earns her own salvation by making me despair. She has sworn not to love, and because of that vow—however it may appear—I am more dead than alive while I tell you this.

BEN: Be advised by me; do not think of her.

ROM: Oh, teach me how I should forget to think then!

BEN: By giving freedom to your eyes. Look on other beauties.

ROM: That will only call her beauty into sharper focus. The black and happy masks that kiss fair ladies' brows remind us that they do hide fair faces. He that is struck blind cannot forget the precious treasure of his lost eyesight. Show me a mistress that is beautiful. Doesn't her beauty serve as a reminder for me to ask who is the one that surpasses that gorgeous creature? Farewell. You cannot teach me to forget.

BEN: I'll teach that lesson to you or die trying. [Exit.]

27

SCENE II
A Street.

[Enter Capulet, Paris, and Servant.]

CAP: But Montague is bound as well as I,
    In penalty alike; and 'tis not hard, I think,
    For men so old as we to keep the peace.

PAR: Of honourable reckoning are you both,
5   And pity 'tis you liv'd at odds so long.
    But now, my lord, what say you to my suit?

CAP: But saying o'er what I have said before:
    My child is yet a stranger in the world,
    She hath not seen the change of fourteen years;
10   Let two more summers wither in their pride
    Ere we may think her ripe to be a bride.

PAR: Younger than she are happy mothers made.

CAP: And too soon marr'd are those so early made.
    The earth hath swallowed all my hopes but she;
15   She is the hopeful lady of my earth.
    But woo her, gentle Paris, get her heart;
    My will to her consent is but a part.
    An she agree, within her scope of choice
    Lies my consent and fair according voice.
20   This night I hold an old accustom'd feast,
    Whereto I have invited many a guest,
    Such as I love; and you among the store,
    One more, most welcome, makes my number more.
    At my poor house look to behold this night
25   Earth-treading stars that make dark heaven light.
    Such comfort as do lusty young men feel
    When well-apparell'd April on the heel
    Of limping Winter treads, even such delight
    Among fresh female buds shall you this night
30   Inherit at my house. Hear all, all see,

SCENE II
A Street.

[Enter Capulet, County Paris, and Servant—the Clown.]

CAP: But Montague is bound as well as I by a similar penalty; and it is not hard, I think, for men as old as we are to keep the peace.

PAR: You both are honorable, and it is a pity you quarreled so long together. But now, my lord, what do you say to my proposition?

CAP: I repeat what I have said before. My child is yet a baby to the world; she is not even fourteen years old. Let two more summers pass before we think her ripe enough to be a bride.

PAR: There are younger than she, who are already happily made mothers.

CAP: And too soon are they also aged. The earth has swallowed all my hopes except her; she is the hope of my earth. But woo her, gentle Paris, gain her heart; my permission will follow her consent. And if she agrees, to her choice I will add my consent and voice. This night I will hold an old customary feast, to which I have invited many guests and friends I love; and you among that group have been added—most welcome—increasing my numbers. At my poor house tonight look to behold beautiful women, earth-treading stars, that can make the dark heaven light up. Such comforts do lusty young men relish when spring comes on the heel of limping winter. Thus, such delights of fresh female buds shall you see this night at my house. Hear all. See all the girls, after which you may like her most whose merits shall be most, which, in review of many, mine being one, Juliet may stand out in number. Come, go with me. [To Servant, giving him a paper] Go, sir. Trudge about through fair Verona; find those persons whose names are written there, and to them say my house and welcome wait on their pleasure. [Exit Capulet and Paris.]

And like her most whose merit most shall be;
Which, amongst view of many, mine, being one,
May stand in number, though in reck'ning none.
Come, go with me. [To Servant, giving him a paper]
35 Go, sirrah, trudge about
Through fair Verona; find those persons out
Whose names are written there, and to them say,
My house and welcome on their pleasure stay.
                    [Exeunt Capulet and Paris.]

SERV: Find them out whose names are written here? It is written that
40 the shoemaker should meddle with his yard and the tailor with his
last, the fisher with his pencil, and the painter with his nets; but I
am sent to find those persons whose names are here writ, and can
never find what names the writing person hath here writ. I must
to the learned. In good time!

[Enter Benvolio and Romeo.]

45 BEN: Tut, man! one fire burns out another's burning;
One pain is lessened by another's anguish;
Turn giddy, and be holp by backward turning;
One desperate grief cures with another's languish.
Take thou some new infection to thy eye,
50 And the rank poison of the old will die.

ROM: Your plantain leaf is excellent for that.

BEN: For what, I pray thee?

ROM: For your broken shin.

BEN: Why, Romeo, art thou mad?

55 ROM: Not mad, but bound more than a madman is;
Shut up in Prison, kept without my food,
Whipp'd and tormented and—God-den, good fellow.

SERV: God gi' god-den. I pray, sir, can you read?

SERV: *Find them out whose names are written here? It is written that the shoe-maker should not leave his yard stick nor the tailor his bench, the fisher his pencil and the painter his nets; but here I am sent to find those persons whose names are here written, and I cannot read the names Capulet has written. I must go to someone who reads.*

[Enter Benvolio and Romeo.]

BEN: *Shoot, man, you know that one fire burns out another; one pain is eased by another's anguish; one laughs when grief is past; one desperate grief is cured by another's lingering disease. So, take some new infection to your eye, and the rank poison of the old will disappear.*

ROM: *Your medicinal leaf is excellent for that.*

BEN: *For what, I ask you?*

ROM: *For your broken shin.*

BEN: *Why, Romeo, are you mad?*

ROM: *Not mad, but more bound in than a madman is; shut up in prison, kept without my food, whipped and tormented and* [To the servant.] *Good evening, good fellow.*

SERV: *God give a good evening. I ask you, sir, can you read?*

ROM: Ay, mine own fortune in my misery.

60   SERV: Perhaps you have learned it without book. But I pray, can you
read any thing you see?

ROM: Ay, If I know the letters and the language.

SERV: Ye say honestly. Rest you merry!

ROM: Stay, fellow; I can read. *[He reads.]*
65   'Signior Martino and his wife and daughters;
County Anselme and his beauteous sisters;
The lady widow of Vitruvio;
Signior Placentio and His lovely nieces;
Mercutio and his brother Valentine;
70   Mine uncle Capulet, his wife, and daughters;
My fair niece Rosaline and Livia;
Signior Valentio and his cousin Tybalt;
Lucio and the lively Helena.' *[Gives back the paper.]*
A fair assembly. Whither should they come?

75   SERV: Up.

ROM: Whither to supper?

SERV: To our house.

ROM: Whose house?

SERV: My master's.

80   ROM: Indeed, I should have ask'd you that before.

SERV: Now I'll tell you without asking. My master is the great rich
Capulet; and if you be not of the house of Montagues, I pray, come
and crush a cup of wine. Rest you merry! *[Exit.]*

BEN: At this same ancient feast of Capulet's
85   Sups the fair Rosaline whom thou so lov'st;
With all the admired beauties of Verona.

ROM: Ay, I can read my own misfortune in my misery.

SERV: Perhaps you have learned it without a book. But I ask you, can you read anything you see?

ROM: Yes, if I know the letters and the language.

SERV: You say honestly. Farewell!

ROM: Wait, fellow; I can read. [He reads.]
"Signior Martino and his wife and daughter; Count Anselme and his beautiful sisters; the lady widow of Vitruvio; Signior Placentio and his lovely nieces; Mercutio and his brother Valentine; my uncle Capulet, his wife, and daughters; my fair niece Rosaline and Livia; Signior Valentio and his cousin Tybalt; Lucio and the lively Helena." [Gives back the paper.] A nice group. Where should they go?

SERV: Up.

ROM: Where do they eat supper?

SERV: At our house.

ROM: Whose house?

SERV: My master's.

ROM: Indeed I should have asked you that before.

SERV: Now, I'll tell you without you asking. My master is the great rich Capulet. If you are not of the house of Montagues, I ask you to come and drink a cup of wine. Good-bye!   [Exit.]

BEN: At this same ancient feast of Capulet's, the fair Rosaline, whom you so love will dine, with all the admired beauties of Verona. Go there, and with clear

Go thither, and with unattainted eye
Compare her face with some that I shall show,
And I will make thee think thy swan a crow.

90 Rom: When the devout religion of mine eye
Maintains such falsehood, then turn tears to fires.
And these, who often drown'd, could never die,
Transparent heretics, be burnt for liars!
One fairer than my love? The all-seeing sun
95 Ne'er saw her match since first the world begun.

Ben: Tut! you saw her fair, none else being by,
Herself pois'd with herself in either eye;
But in that crystal scales let there be weigh'd
Your lady's love against some other maid
100 That I will show you shining at this feast,
And she shall scant show well that now seems best.

Rom: I'll go along, no such sight to be shown,
But to rejoice in splendour of my own.

                                        [Exeunt.]

eyes, compare her face with some that I shall point out to you, and I will make you think your swan is a crow.

ROM: When my eyes support such falsehood, then may my tears turn to fires. And even though my eyes have cried drowning tears, they should burn if they lie and see anyone other than Rosaline. Someone fairer than my love? The all-seeing sun never saw her equal since the world first began.

BEN: Nonsense! You've only seen her beauty when no one else was there; you see her flanked only with herself in both your eyes. But use those crystal scales to weigh your lady's love against some other maiden whom I will show you shining at this feast; your lady who now seems the best will no longer seem the best.

ROM: I'll go along, but no such sight will I be shown; instead, I will rejoice in my own beloved Rosaline.   [Exit.]

SCENE III
Capulet's House.

[Enter Lady Capulet, and Nurse.]

LADY CAP: Nurse, where's my daughter? Call her forth to me.

NURSE: Now, by my maidenhead at twelve year old, I bade her come.
What, lamb! what ladybird! God forbid! Where's this girl? What,
Juliet!

[Enter Juliet.]

5   JUL: How now? Who calls?

NURSE: Your mother.

JUL: Madam, I am here.
What is your will?

LADY CAP: This is the matter—Nurse, give leave awhile,
10   We must talk in secret. Nurse, come back again;
I have remenber'd me, thou shalt hear our counsel.
Thou knowest my daughter's of a pretty age.

NURSE: Faith, I can tell her age unto an hour.

LADY CAP: She's not fourteen.

15   NURSE: I'll lay fourteen of my teeth-
And yet, to my teen be it spoken, I have but four-
She is not fourteen. How long is it now
To Lammastide?

LADY CAP: A fortnight and odd days.

20   NURSE: Even or odd, of all days in the year,
Come Lammas Eve at night shall she be fourteen.
Susan and she (God rest all Christian souls!)

SCENE III
Capulet's House.

[Enter Lady Capulet, and Nurse.]

LADY CAP: *Nurse, where's my daughter? Call her forth to me.*

NURSE: *Now, by my virginity at twelve years old, I bid her to come. Here, lamb! Here, ladybird! Heaven forbid, where has this girl gone? Juliet!*

[Enter Juliet.]

JUL: *What's this? Who calls?*

NURSE: *Your mother.*

JUL: *Madam, I am here. What is your will?*

LADY CAP: *This is the matter—Nurse, leave us awhile, we must talk in secret. Nurse, come back again. I have remembered; you hear our counsel. You know my daughter is of a tender age.*

NURSE: *Yes, I can tell her age within an hour.*

LADY CAP: *She's not yet fourteen.*

NURSE: *I'll bet fourteen of my teeth—and yet, to my sorrow, I have only four left—that she is not fourteen. How long is it till August 1ˢᵗ?*

LADY CAP: *Two weeks and a few days.*

NURSE: *Come July 31ˢᵗ, she shall be fourteen. Susan and she (God rest all Christian souls!) were of similar years. Well, Susan is with God; she was too good for me. But, as I said, on Lammas Eve at night she shall be fourteen—*

Were of an age. Well, Susan is with God;
She was too good for me. But, as I said,
25   On Lammas Eve at night shall she be fourteen;
That shall she, marry; I remember it well.
'Tis since the earthquake now eleven years;
And she was wean'd (I never shall forget it),
Of all the days of the year, upon that day;
30   For I had then laid wormwood to my dug,
Sitting in the sun under the dovehouse wall.
My lord and you were then at Mantua.
Nay, I do bear a brain. But, as I said,
When it did taste the wormwood on the nipple
35   Of my dug and felt it bitter, pretty fool,
To see it tetchy and fall out with the dug!
Shake, quoth the dovehouse! 'Twas no need, I trow,
To bid me trudge.
And since that time it is eleven years,
40   For then she could stand high-lone; nay, by th' rood,
She could have run and waddled all about;
 For even the day before, she broke her brow;
And then my husband (God be with his soul!
A' was a merry man) took up the child.
45   'Yea,' quoth he, 'dost thou fall upon thy face?
Thou wilt fall backward when thou hast more wit;
Wilt thou not, Jule?' and, by my holidame,
The pretty wretch left crying, and said 'Ay.'
To see now how a jest shall come about!
50   I warrant, an I should live a thousand years,
I never should forget it. 'Wilt thou not, Jule?' quoth he,
And, pretty fool, it stinted, and said 'Ay.'

LADY CAP: Enough of this. I pray thee hold thy peace.

NURSE: Yes, madam. Yet I cannot choose but laugh
55   To think it should leave crying and say 'Ay.'
And yet, I warrant, it had upon it brow
A bump as big as a young cock'rel's stone;
A perilous knock; and it cried bitterly.
Yea,' quoth my husband, 'fall'st upon thy face?
60   Thou wilt fall backward when thou comest to age;
Wilt thou not, Jule?' It stinted, and said 'Ay.'

38

that shall she be. Yes; I remember it well. It is since the earthquake eleven years now; and she was weaned (I never shall forget it) of all the days of the year upon that day; for I had then put bitter juice on my breast, sitting in the sun under the dovehouse wall. My lord and you were then at Mantua. Yes, I do have a memory. But, as I said, when she tasted the wormwood on the nipple of my breast and thought it bitter, pretty fool; we saw her fretful and leave the breast! Time to leave! It wasn't necessary to tell me to go leave her, and since that time, it is now eleven years, for then she could stand alone; nay, by the cross, she could have run and waddled all about. Even the day before, she cut her forehead, and then my husband (God be with his soul! He was a merry man!) took Juliet up. "Yes," says he, "do you fall upon your face? You will fall on your back when you have more sense; will you not, Jule?" And, by my holiness, the pretty wretch stopped crying, and said "Yes." It's easy to see now how a joke shall come true! I believe if I should live a thousand years I never should forget it. "Will you not, Jule?" says he, and, pretty fool, she stopped, and said, "Yes."

LADY CAP: *Enough of this. I ask you hold your tongue.*

NURSE: *Yes, madam. Yet I cannot help but laugh to think she should stop crying and say, "Yes." And yet, I believe, she had upon her brow a bump as big as a young rooster's stone; a perilous knock, and she cried bitterly. "Yes," says my husband, "fall upon your face? You will fall on your back when you come of age; will you not, Jule?" She stopped crying, and said, "Yes."*

JUL: And stint thou too, I pray thee, Nurse, say I.

NURSE: Peace, I have done. God mark thee to his grace!
    Thou wast the prettiest babe that e'er I nurs'd.
65   An I might live to see thee married once, I have my wish.

LADY CAP: Marry, that 'marry' is the very theme
    I came to talk of. Tell me, daughter Juliet,
    How stands your disposition to be married?

JUL: It is an honour that I dream not of.

70   NURSE: An honour? Were not I thine only Nurse,
    I would say thou hadst suck'd wisdom from thy teat.

LADY CAP: Well, think of marriage now. Younger than you,
    Here in Verona, ladies of esteem,
    Are made already mothers. By my count,
75   I was your mother much upon these years
    That you are now a maid. Thus then in brief:
    The valiant Paris seeks you for his love.

NURSE: A man, young lady! lady, such a man
    As all the world—why he's a man of wax.

80   LADY CAP: Verona's summer hath not such a flower.

NURSE: Nay, he's a flower, in faith- a very flower.

LADY CAP: What say you? Can you love the gentleman?
    This night you shall behold him at our feast.
    Read o'er the volume of young Paris' face,
85   And find delight writ there with beauty's pen;
    Examine every married lineament,
    And see how one another lends content;
    And what obscur'd in this fair volume lies
    Find written in the margent of his eyes,
90   This precious book of love, this unbound lover,
    To beautify him only lacks a cover.

JUL: *Stop this, too. Please, Nurse,*

NURSE: *Shush, I am done. God take you to His grace! You were the prettiest babe that ever I nursed. And if I might live to see you married once, I would have my wish.*

LADY CAP: *God, that "marry" is the very theme I came to talk about. Tell me, daughter Juliet, how do you feel about being married?*

JUL: *It is an honor that I do not dream of.*

NURSE: *An honor? Were I not your only Nurse I would say that you had sucked wisdom from the breast.*

LADY CAP: *Well, think of marriage now. Younger girls than you, right here in Verona, and ladies of esteem, are already made mothers. By my count, I was the same age you are now when I became your mother. Thus then, briefly; the valiant Paris seeks you for his bride.*

NURSE: *A man, young lady! Lady, such a man as any in the world—why he's as handsome as a wax figure.*

LADY CAP: *Verona's summer has not seen such a flower.*

NURSE: *No, he's a flower, to be sure—a very flower.*

LADY CAP: *What do you say? Can you love the gentleman? This night you shall see him at our feast. Read over young Paris' face and find delight written there with beauty's pen. Examine every balanced line and see how every line makes a perfect whole and discover what is obscure in this fair volume written in the margin of his eyes. This precious book of love, this unbound lover: he only lacks a cover to make him perfect. For some people, that book shares a glory with books done in golden clasps that lock in a golden story. So shall you share all that he does possess, and by having him you make yourself no less a person.*

41

The fish lives in the sea, and 'tis much pride
For fair without the fair within to hide.
That book in many's eyes doth share the glory,
95   That in gold clasps locks in the golden story;
So shall you share all that he doth possess,
By having him making yourself no less.

NURSE: No less? Nay, bigger! Women grow by men.

LADY CAP: Speak briefly, can you like of Paris' love?

100   JUL: I'll look to like, if looking liking move;
But no more deep will I endart mine eye
Than your consent gives strength to make it fly.

[Enter Servingman.]

SERV: Madam, the guests are come, supper serv'd up, you call'd, my
young lady ask'd for, the Nurse curs'd in the pantry, and everything
105   in extremity. I must hence to wait. I beseech you follow straight.

LADY CAP: We follow thee.   *[Exit Servingman.]*
Juliet, the County stays.

NURSE: Go, girl, seek happy nights to happy days.
                                        [Exeunt.]

NURSE: No less? Nay, bigger! Women grow pregnant by men.

LADY CAP: Speak briefly; can you accept Paris' love?

JUL: I'll look at him to see if I like him; if my looking makes me like him, I'll go no further than your consent gives me the permission to go.

[Enter Servingman.]

SERV: Madam, the guests have come, and supper is served. They are calling for you and the young lady; the Nurse is being cursed in the pantry, and everything is chaos. I must go to wait on the guests. I beg you to follow immediately.

LADY CAP: We follow you.   [Exit Servingman.]
  Juliet, Paris waits.

NURSE: Go, girl, seek happy nights and happy days.   [Exit.]

SCENE IV

A street.

[*Enter Romeo, Mercutio, Benvolio, with five or six other Maskers; Torchbearers.*]

ROM: What, shall this speech be spoke for our excuse?
    Or shall we on without apology?

BEN: The date is out of such prolixity.
    We'll have no Cupid hoodwink'd with a scarf,
5   Bearing a Tartar's painted bow of lath,
    Scaring the ladies like a crowkeeper;
    Nor no without-book prologue, faintly spoke
    After the prompter, for our entrance;
    But, let them measure us by what they will,
10   We'll measure them a measure, and be gone.

ROM: Give me a torch. I am not for this ambling.
    Being but heavy, I will bear the light.

MER: Nay, gentle Romeo, we must have you dance.

ROM: Not I, believe me. You have dancing shoes
15   With nimble soles; I have a soul of lead
    So stakes me to the ground I cannot move.

MER: You are a lover. Borrow Cupid's wings
    And soar with them above a common bound.

ROM: I am too sore enpierced with his shaft
20   To soar with his light feathers; and so bound
    I cannot bound a pitch above dull woe.
    Under love's heavy burden do I sink.

MER: And, to sink in it, should you burden love—
    Too great oppression for a tender thing.

25 ROM: Is love a tender thing? It is too rough,
    Too rude, too boist'rous, and it pricks like thorn.

SCENE IV
A street.

[Enter Romeo, Mercutio, Benvolio, with five or six other Maskers; Torchbearers.]

ROM: [Holding a sheet of paper.] *Well, shall this speech be spoken as our excuse, or shall we just enter without apology?*

BEN: *To enter with a speech is unfashionable now. We'll have no masked Cupid, bearing a Tartar's painted bow, scaring the ladies, nor will we use a memorized prologue, faintly spoken after the prompter, to gain our entrance. Let them measure us whatever way they will; we'll only do them a dance and be gone.*

ROM: *Give me a torch. Given my heavy heart, I am not up for this trip. Being only moody, I will bear our light.*

MER: *No, gentle Romeo, we must have you dance.*

ROM: *Not I, believe me. You have dancing shoes with nimble soles; I have a soul of lead which stakes me to the ground so I cannot move.*

MER: *You are a lover. Borrow Cupid's wings and soar with them above a common leap.*

ROM: *I am too sorely pierced with his shaft of love to soar with his light feathers; and thus bound up so, I cannot jump a height above dull woes. Under love's heavy burden do I thus sink.*

MER: *And, sink in it you will, if you burden love—it is too great a weight for such a tender thing.*

ROM: *Is love a tender thing? It is too rough, too rude, too boisterous; and it pricks like thorns.*

45

MER: If love be rough with you, be rough with love.
　　Prick love for pricking, and you beat love down.
　　Give me a case to put my visage in.
30　　A visor for a visor! What care I
　　What curious eye doth quote deformities?
　　Here are the beetle brows shall blush for me.

BEN: Come, knock and enter; and no sooner in
　　But every man betake him to his legs.

35　ROM: A torch for me! Let wantons light of heart
　　Tickle the senseless rushes with their heels;
　　For I am proverb'd with a grandsire phrase,
　　I'll be a candle-holder and look on;
　　The game was ne'er so fair, and I am done.

40　MER: Tut! dun's the mouse, the constable's own word!
　　If thou art dun, we'll draw thee from the mire
　　Or (save your reverence) love, wherein thou stick'st
　　Up to the ears. Come, we burn daylight, ho!

ROM: Nay, that's not so.

45　MER: I mean, sir, in delay
　　We waste our lights in vain, like lamps by day.
　　Take our good meaning, for our judgment sits
　　Five times in that ere once in our five wits.

ROM: And we mean well, in going to this mask;
50　　But 'tis no wit to go.

MER: Why, may one ask?

ROM: I dreamt a dream to-night.

MER: And so did I.

ROM: Well, what was yours?

55　MER: That dreamers often lie.

46

MER: *If love is rough with you, you be rough with love. Prick love for pricking you, and you can beat love down. Give me a mask to put my face in. A mask for an ugly face! Do I care whose curious eyes look at these deformities? Here are beetle brows that shall blush for me.*

BEN: *Come, we will knock and enter. When we are safely inside, every man should go his separate way.*

ROM: *A torch for me! Let others who are light of heart tickle the floor with their heels. I am comforted by the old proverb and will be the watcher and look on; the game was never so fair, and I am satisfied.*

MER: *No! Be still! If you are the dun horse, we'll draw you from the mire of this dung of love where you are stuck up to the ears. Come, we waste time!*

ROM: *No, that's not so.*

MER: *I mean, sir, in delaying, we waste our lights in vain, like lighting lamps by day. Take our good meaning, for our judgment sits five times better in that explanation rather than once in being clever.*

ROM: *And we mean well, in going to this dance; but it is no game to go.*

MER: *Why, may one ask?*

ROM: *I dreamed a dream tonight.*

MER: *And so did I.*

ROM: *Well, what was yours?*

MER: *That dreamers often lie.*

Rom: In bed asleep, while they do dream things true.

Mer: O, then I see Queen Mab hath been with you.
She is the fairies' midwife, and she comes
In shape no bigger than an agate stone
60 On the forefinger of an alderman,
Drawn with a team of little atomies
Athwart men's noses as they lie asleep;
Her wagon spokes made of long spinners' legs,
The cover, of the wings of grasshoppers;
65 Her traces, of the smallest spider's web;
Her collars, of the moonshine's wat'ry beams;
Her whip, of cricket's bone; the lash, of film;
Her wagoner, a small grey-coated gnat,
Not half so big as a round little worm
70 Prick'd from the lazy finger of a maid;
Her chariot is an empty hazelnut,
Made by the joiner squirrel or old grub,
Time out o' mind the fairies' coachmakers.
And in this state she 'gallops night by night
75 Through lovers' brains, and then they dream of love;
O'er courtiers' knees, that dream on court'sies straight;
O'er lawyers' fingers, who straight dream on fees;
O'er ladies' lips, who straight on kisses dream,
Which oft the angry Mab with blisters plagues,
80 Because their breaths with sweetmeats tainted are.
Sometime she gallops o'er a courtier's nose,
And then dreams he of smelling out a suit;
And sometime comes she with a tithe-pig's tail
Tickling a parson's nose as a' lies asleep,
85 Then dreams he of another benefice.
Sometimes she driveth o'er a soldier's neck,
And then dreams he of cutting foreign throats,
Of breaches, ambuscadoes, Spanish blades,
Of healths five fathom deep; and then anon
90 Drums in his ear, at which he starts and wakes,
And being thus frighted, swears a prayer or two
And sleeps again. This is that very Mab
That plats the manes of horses in the night
And bakes the elflocks in foul sluttish hairs,

ROM: *In bed asleep, while they do dream true things.*

MER: *Oh, then I see the fairy queen has been with you. She is the fairies' midwife, and she comes in a shape no bigger than an agate stone on the forefinger of an alderman, drawn with a team of little beings across men's noses as they lie asleep. Her wagon spokes are made of long spiders' legs; the cover, of the wings of grasshoppers; her braces, of the smallest spider's web; her collars, of the moonshine's watery beams; her whip, of cricket's bone; the lash, of vapor; her driver, a small grey-coated gnat, not half so big as a round little worm pricked from the lazy finger of a maid; her chariot is an empty hazelnut, made by the carpenter squirrel or an old grub; time out of mind the fairies' coachmakers. And in this way, she gallops night after night through lovers' brains, and then they dream of love; over courtiers' knees, that dream of curt-sies straight away; over lawyers' fingers, who mostly dream about fees; over ladies' lips, who dream about kisses and who Mab often plagues with blisters because their breaths are tainted with sweetmeats. Sometimes, she gallops over a courtier's nose, and then he dreams of winning a suit; and sometimes, she comes with a pig's tail tickling a parson's nose as he lies asleep, and then he dreams of another gift. Sometimes, she drives over a soldier's neck, and then he dreams of cutting foreign throats, of breaches, of ambushes, of Spanish blades, of toasts five fathoms deep; and then at once, he hears drums in his ear, which startle and wake him; and being thus frightened, he swears a prayer or two and sleeps again. This is that very Mab that twists the manes of horses in the night and mats their hair into sloppy tangles, which, when untangled, causes misfortune for men. This is the hag, when maids lie on their backs, who presses them and teaches them now to bear children, making them women of good carriage. This is she—*

95   Which once untangled much misfortune bodes
        This is the hag, when maids lie on their backs,
        That presses them and learns them first to bear,
        Making them women of good carriage.
        This is she—

100   ROM: Peace, peace, Mercutio, peace!
        Thou talk'st of nothing.

        MER: True, I talk of dreams;
        Which are the children of an idle brain,
        Begot of nothing but vain fantasy;
105   Which is as thin of substance as the air,
        And more inconstant than the wind, who wooes
        Even now the frozen bosom of the north
        And, being anger'd, puffs away from thence,
        Turning his face to the dew-dropping south.

110   BEN: This wind you talk of blows us from ourselves.
        Supper is done, and we shall come too late.

        ROM: I fear, too early; for my mind misgives
        Some consequence, yet hanging in the stars,
        Shall bitterly begin his fearful date
115   With this night's revels and expire the term
        Of a despised life, clos'd in my breast,
        By some vile forfeit of untimely death.
        But He, that hath the steerage of my course,
        Direct my sail! On, lusty gentlemen!

120   BEN: Strike, drum.

        [They march about the stage. Exeunt.]

ROM: *Stop, stop, Mercutio, peace! You talk about nothing.*

MER: *True, I talk of dreams which are the children of only idle brains, begun by nothing but vain fantasy. It is as thin a substance as the air is and more inconstant than the wind, who woos even now the frozen bosom of the north and, being angered, puffs away from there, turning his face to the dew-dropping south.*

BEN: *This wind you talk of blows us from our purposes. Supper is done, and we shall arrive too late.*

ROM: *I fear too early; for my mind worries about some consequence, already fated by the stars, shall bitterly begin his fearful time with this night's revels and end the term of a despised life by some wicked payment of untimely death. But God is steering my course, directing my sail! On, lusty gentlemen!*

BEN: *Strike, drum.*

[They march about the stage. Exit.]

SCENE V
Capulet's House.

[Servingmen come forth with napkins.]

1. SERV: Where's Potpan, that he helps not to take away?
   He shift a trencher! he scrape a trencher!

2. SERV: When good manners shall lie all in one or two men's hands,
and they unwash'd too, 'tis a foul thing.

5   1 SERV: Away with the joint-stools, remove the court-cupboard, look
to the plate. Good thou, save me a piece of marchpane and, as thou
lovest me, let the porter let in Susan Grindstone and Nell.
Anthony, and Potpan!

2. SERV: Ay, boy, ready.

[Enter Third and Fourth servants.]

10   1 SERV: You are look'd for and call'd for, ask'd for and sought for, in
          the great chamber.

3. SERV: We cannot be here and there too. Cheerly, boys!
   Be brisk awhile, and the longer liver take all.   *[Exeunt.]*

[Enter the Maskers, Enter, (with Servants) Capulet, his Wife, Juliet,
15   *Tybalt, and all the Guests and Gentlewomen to the Maskers.]*

CAP: Welcome, gentlemen! Ladies that have their toes
          Unplagu'd with corns will have a bout with you.
          Ah ha, my mistresses! which of you all
          Will now deny to dance? She that makes dainty,
20   She, I'll swear, hath corns. Am I come near ye now?
          Welcome, gentlemen! I have seen the day
          That I have worn a visor and could tell
          A whispering tale in a fair lady's ear,
          Such as would please. 'Tis gone, 'tis gone, 'tis gone!
25   You are welcome, gentlemen! Come, musicians, play.

SCENE V
Capulet's House.

[Servingmen come forth with napkins.]

1. SERV: Where's Potpan that he does not help take things away? He moves a platter! He scrapes a platter!

2. SERV: When good jobs are done only by one or two men's hands, and those unwashed, too, it is a foul thing.

1. SERV: Away with the folding stools; remove the court-cupboard; watch the silver. Save me a piece of dessert and, if you love me, tell the porter to let in Susan Grindstone and Nell. [Calls to.] Anthony and Potpan!

2. SERV: Yes, boy, ready.

[Enter Third and Fourth servants.]

1. SERV: You are looked for and called for, asked for and sought for in the great chamber.

3. SERV: We cannot be here and there too.Cheerily, boys! Be brisk awhile, and the one who lives longest will take all.   [Exit.]

[Enter the Maskers; Enter with Servants Capulet, his Wife, Juliet, Tybalt, and all the Guests and Gentlewomen to the Maskers.]

CAP: Welcome, gentlemen! Ladies that have their toes free of corns will have a dance with you. Ah, ha, my mistresses! Which of you all will now deny to dance? She that acts shyly I'll swear has corns. Have I come close to the truth? Welcome, gentlemen! I have seen the day that I have also worn a mask and told a whispering tale in a fair lady's ear, such as would please her. It is gone, it is gone, it is gone! You are welcome, gentlemen! Come, musicians, play. Clear the floor! Give us room! And dance, girls.

A hall, a hall! give room! and foot it, girls.
[Music plays, and they dance.]
More light, you knaves! and turn the tables up,
And quench the fire, the room is grown too hot.
Ah, sirrah, this unlook'd-for sport comes well.
30   Nay, sit, nay, sit, good cousin Capulet,
For you and I are past our dancing days.
How long is't now since last yourself and I
Were in a mask?

2. CAP: By'r Lady, thirty years.

35   CAP: What, man? 'Tis not so much, 'tis not so much!
'Tis since the nuptial of Lucentio,
Come Pentecost as quickly as it will,
Some five-and-twenty years, and then we mask'd.

2. CAP: 'Tis more, 'tis more! His son is elder, sir;
40   His son is thirty.

CAP: Will you tell me that?
His son was but a ward two years ago.

ROM: *[To a Servingman.]* What lady's that, which doth enrich the hand
45   Of yonder knight?

SERV: I know not, sir.

ROM: O, she doth teach the torches to burn bright!
It seems she hangs upon the cheek of night
Like a rich jewel in an Ethiop's ear—
50   Beauty too rich for use, for earth too dear!
So shows a snowy dove trooping with crows
As yonder lady o'er her fellows shows.
The measure done, I'll watch her place of stand
And, touching hers, make blessed my rude hand.
55   Did my heart love till now? Forswear it, sight!
For I ne'er saw true beauty till this night.

54

[Music plays, and they dance.]
More light, you fools! Move the tables, and quench the fire; the room has grown too hot. Ah, sir, this unlooked for sport goes well. No, sit. Sit, good cousin Capulet, for you and I are past our dancing days. How long is it now since you and I were at such a party?

2. CAP: By your Lady, thirty years.

CAP: What, man? It can't be so much; it is not long! It was at the wedding of Lucentio, some five-and-twenty years ago that we partied.

2. CAP: It is more; it is more! His son is older, sir; his son is thirty.

CAP: Is that really so? His son was still a child only two years ago.

ROM: [To a Servingman.] What lady is that who holds the hand of that man?

SERV: I don't know, sir.

ROM: Oh, she teaches the torches to burn brightly! It seems she hangs upon the cheek of night like a rich jewel in an African's ear—beauty too rich for use, it is too dear for earth! The lady over there appears much prettier than her friends; she looks like a snowy dove surrounded by crows. The dance is done, so I'll watch where she stands and, by touching her hand, she will make my rough hand blessed. Did my heart ever love until now? My eyes will swear that I never saw true beauty until this night.

TYB: This, by his voice, should be a Montague.
    Fetch me my rapier, boy. What, dares the slave
    Come hither, cover'd with an antic face,
60   To fleer and scorn at our solemnity?
    Now, by the stock and honour of my kin,
    To strike him dead I hold it not a sin.

CAP: Why, how now, kinsman? Wherefore storm you so?

TYB: Uncle, this is a Montague, our foe;
65   A villain, that is hither come in spite
    To scorn at our solemnity this night.

CAP: Young Romeo is it?

TYB: 'Tis he, that villain Romeo.

CAP: Content thee, gentle coz, let him alone.
70   He bears him like a portly gentleman,
    And, to say truth, Verona brags of him
    To be a virtuous and well-govern'd youth.
    I would not for the wealth of all this town
    Here in my house do him disparagement.
75   Therefore be patient, take no note of him.
    It is my will; the which if thou respect,
    Show a fair presence and put off these frowns,
    An ill-beseeming semblance for a feast.

TYB: It fits when such a villain is a guest.
80   I'll not endure him.

CAP: He shall be endur'd.
    What, goodman boy? I say he shall. Go to!
    Am I the master here, or you? Go to!
    You'll not endure him? God shall mend my soul!
85   You'll make a mutiny among my guests!
    You will set cock-a-hoop! you'll be the man!

TYB: Why, uncle, 'tis a shame.

TYB: This, by his voice, should be a Montague. Fetch me my rapier, boy. What! Does the slave dare to come here, covered with a grotesque mask, to mock and scorn at our festival? Now, by the stock and honor of my relatives, I would not hold it a sin to strike him dead.

CAP: Why, what, kinsman? What upsets you so?

TYB: Uncle, [Pointing.] this is a Montague, our foe; he is a villain who has come here to spite our party this night.

CAP: Young Romeo, is it?

TYB: It is he, that villain Romeo.

CAP: Ease up, gentle cousin, let him alone. He bears himself like a good gentleman; and, to say the truth, Verona brags of him to be a virtuous and well-governed youth. I would not for the wealth of all this town do him wrong here in my house. Therefore be patient; take no note of him. It is my desire that you respect my wish by showing a fair presence and putting off these frowns, which are not appropriate for a feast.

TYB: They're appropriate when such a villain is a guest. I'll not endure him.

CAP: He shall be endured. Do you hear that, boy? I say he shall. Do it! Am I the master here, or you? Do it! You'll not endure him? God bless my soul! You'll cause a fight among my guests! And start a fight just so you could be the man!

TYB: Why, uncle, it is shameful.

CAP: Go to, go to!
    You are a saucy boy. Is't so, indeed?
90   This trick may chance to scathe you. I know what.
    You must contrary me! You are a princox—go!
    Be quiet, or—More light, more light!—For shame!
    I'll make you quiet; what!—Cheerly, my hearts!

TYB: Patience perforce with wilful choler meeting
95   Makes my flesh tremble in their different greeting.
    I will withdraw; but this intrusion shall,
    Now seeming sweet, convert to bitt'rest gall.   *[Exit.]*

ROM: If I profane with my unworthiest hand
    This holy shrine, the gentle fine is this:
100   My lips, two blushing pilgrims, ready stand
    To smooth that rough touch with a tender kiss.

JUL: Good pilgrim, you do wrong your hand too much,
    Which mannerly devotion shows in this;
    For saints have hands that pilgrims' hands do touch,
105   And palm to palm is holy palmers' kiss.

ROM: Have not saints lips, and holy palmers too?

JUL: Ay, pilgrim, lips that they must use in prayer.

ROM: O, then, dear saint, let lips do what hands do!
    They pray; grant thou, lest faith turn to despair.

110 JUL: Saints do not move, though grant for prayers' sake.

ROM: Then move not while my prayer's effect I take.
    Thus from my lips, by thine my sin is purg'd.   *[Kisses her.]*

JUL: Then have my lips the sin that they have took.

ROM: Sin from my lips? O trespass sweetly urg'd!
115   Give me my sin again.   *[Kisses her.]*

JUL: You kiss by th' book.

CAP: Do it; do it! You are a cheeky boy. Is it so, indeed? I know that if you act contrary to my wishes, such a trick may chance to harm you. —You are insulting—go! Be quiet or—more light, more light!—For shame! Keep quiet or I'll make you quiet;—Cheerily, my hearts!

TYB: Patience joined with anger mixes strangely; it makes my flesh tremble in their different greetings. I will withdraw; but this intrusion, which now seems sweet, will convert to bitterest feeling.   [Exit.]

ROM: If I profane with my unworthy hand, this holy shrine, my lips, these two blushing pilgrims, stand ready to smooth that rough touch with a tender kiss.

JUL: Good pilgrim, you do too strongly wrong your hand which has only shown mannerly devotion; for statues have hands that are touched by pilgrims' hands, and by placing palm to palm is the way holy pilgrims kiss.

ROM: Do not saints have lips, and holy pilgrims too?

JUL: Ay, pilgrim, lips that they must use in prayer.

ROM: Oh, then, dear saint, let my lips do what hands do! Since hands pray, may you grant my prayer, lest my faith turns to despair.

JUL: Though they answer prayers, saints do not move.

ROM: Then do not move while I see the effect of my prayers. Thus from my lips, my sin is purged by a kiss from your lips. [Kisses her.]

JUL: So my lips have the sin that they have taken from you.

ROM: Sin from my lips? O sin sweetly urged! Give me back my sin. [Kisses her.]

JUL: You kiss by the book.

NURSE: Madam, your mother craves a word with you.

ROM: What is her mother?

NURSE: Marry, bachelor,
120   Her mother is the lady of the house.
        And a good lady, and a wise and virtuous.
        I nurs'd her daughter that you talk'd withal.
        I tell you, he that can lay hold of her
        Shall have the chinks.

125   ROM: Is she a Capulet?
        O dear account! my life is my foe's debt.

BEN: Away, be gone; the sport is at the best.

ROM: Ay, so I fear; the more is my unrest.

CAP: Nay, gentlemen, prepare not to be gone;
130   We have a trifling foolish banquet towards.
        Is it e'en so? Why then, I thank you all.
        I thank you, honest gentlemen. Good night.
        More torches here!   [Exeunt Maskers.]
        Come on then, let's to bed.
135   Ah, sirrah, by my fay, it waxes late;
        I'll to my rest.
                    [Exeunt all but Juliet and Nurse.]

JUL: Come hither, Nurse. What is yon gentleman?

NURSE: The son and heir of old Tiberio.

JUL: What's he that now is going out of door?

140   NURSE: Marry, that, I think, be young Petruchio.

JUL: What's he that follows there, that would not dance?

NURSE: I know not.

60

NURSE: *Madam, your mother craves a word with you.*

ROM: *Who is her mother?*

NURSE: *Well, son, her mother is the lady of the house. And a good lady, and a wise and virtuous one. I nursed her daughter whom you talked with. I tell you, he that can lay hold of her shall have the world.*

ROM: *Is she a Capulet? Oh, dear account! My life is in my foe's hands.*

BEN: *Away, let's go; we've had a great time.*

ROM: *Ay, so I fear greater will be my undoing.*

CAP: *No, gentlemen, do not leave. We have a small foolish banquet coming. Is it so? Why then, I thank you all. I thank you, honest gentlemen. Good night. More torches here!* [Exit Maskers.] *Come on then, let's go to bed. Ah, sir, by my faith, it's getting late; I'll go to my rest.*
[Exit all but Juliet and Nurse.]

JUL: *Come here, Nurse. Who is that gentleman?*

NURSE: *The son and heir of old Tiberio.*

JUL: *Who's that who now is going out of the door?*

NURSE: *Well, that, I think, is young Petruchio.*

JUL: *Who's that who follows there, the man who would not dance?*

NURSE: *I don't know.*

JUL: Go ask his name.—If he be married,
My grave is like to be my wedding bed.

145 NURSE: His name is Romeo, and a Montague,
The only son of your great enemy.

JUL: My only love, sprung from my only hate!
Too early seen unknown, and known too late!
Prodigious birth of love it is to me
150 That I must love a loathed enemy.

NURSE: What's this? what's this?

JUL: A rhyme I learn'ds even now
Of one I danc'd withal.
[One calls within, 'Juliet.']

155 NURSE: Anon, anon!
Come, let's away; the strangers all are gone. *[Exeunt.]*

JUL: *Go ask his name. If he is married, my grave is likely to be my wedding bed.*

NURSE: [Returns] *His name is Romeo, and a Montague, the only son of your great enemy.*

JUL: *Sprung from my only hate is my only love. Too early seen and known too late! My birth is so fickle that I must love a loathed enemy.*

NURSE: *What's this? What's this?*

JUL: *A rhyme I learned even now of one I danced with.*

[One calls within "Juliet"]

NURSE: *Yes, yes! Come, let's away; the strangers all are gone.*   [Exit.]

ACT II

PROLOGUE

[Enter Chorus.]

CHOR: Now old desire doth in his deathbed lie,
    And young affection gapes to be his heir;
    That fair for which love groan'd for and would die,
    With tender Juliet match'd, is now not fair.
5   Now Romeo is belov'd, and loves again,
    Alike bewitched by the charm of looks;
    But to his foe suppos'd he must complain,
    And she steal love's sweet bait from fearful hooks.
    Being held a foe, he may not have access
10   To breathe such vows as lovers use to swear,
    And she as much in love, her means much less
    To meet her new beloved anywhere;
    But passion lends them power, time means, to meet,
    Temp'ring extremities with extreme sweet.   *[Exit.]*

ACT II

PROLOGUE

[Enter Chorus.]

Chor: *Now, old desire lies in his deathbed, and young affection wishes to be his heir; Rosaline, for whose love Romeo groaned and would die, is now not fair when compared with Juliet. Now, Romeo is beloved and loves again; both he and Juliet are bewitched by the charm of looks. But to his supposed foe, he must speak love while she steals love's sweet bait from fearful hooks. Being held a foe, he may not have access to speak such vows as lovers typically swear. She also is in love and has even less opportunities also to meet her new beloved anywhere: Passion lends them power, time, and the means to meet, tempering harshness with extreme sweetness.* [Exit.]

SCENE I

A lane by the wall of Capulet's orchard.

[Enter Romeo alone.]

ROM: Can I go forward when my heart is here?
　　Turn back, dull earth, and find thy centre out.

[Climbs the wall and leaps down within it.]

[Enter Benvolio with Mercutio.]

BEN: Romeo! my cousin Romeo! Romeo!

MER: He is wise,
5　　And, on my life, hath stol'n him home to bed.

BEN: He ran this way, and leapt this orchard wall.
　　Call, good Mercutio.

MER: Nay, I'll conjure too.
　　Romeo! humours! madman! passion! lover!
10　　Appear thou in the likeness of a sigh;
　　Speak but one rhyme, and I am satisfied!
　　Cry but 'Ay me!' pronounce but 'love' and 'dove';
　　Speak to my gossip Venus one fair word,
　　One nickname for her purblind son and heir,
15　　Young Adam Cupid, he that shot so trim
　　When King Cophetua lov'd the beggar maid!
　　He heareth not, he stirreth not, be moveth not;
　　The ape is dead, and I must conjure him.
　　I conjure thee by Rosaline's bright eyes.
20　　By her high forehead and her scarlet lip,
　　By her fine foot, straight leg, and quivering thigh,
　　And the demesnes that there adjacent lie,
　　That in thy likeness thou appear to us!

BEN: An if he hear thee, thou wilt anger him.

SCENE I

A lane by the wall of Capulet's orchard.

[Enter Romeo alone.]

ROM: *Can I go forward when my heart is here? Turn back, dull earth, and find your center.*

[Climbs the wall and leaps down within it.]

[Enter Benvolio with Mercutio.]

BEN: *Romeo! My cousin Romeo! Romeo!*

MER: *He is wise and, on my life, has stolen himself home to bed.*

BEN: *He ran this way and leaped over this orchard wall. Call, good Mercutio.*

MER: *No, I'll conjure his spirit.* [Calls aloud.] *Romeo! Moods! Madman! Passion! Lover! Appear in the likeness of a sigh; speak but one rhyme, and I am satisfied! Cry, "Oh me!" pronounce "love" and "dove"; speak one fair word to my friend Venus, one nickname for her weak-sighted son and heir, young Cupid: he who shot so neatly when King Cophetua loved the beggar maid! Romeo heard not, he stirred not, he moved not; the boy is dead, and I must conjure him again by Rosaline's bright eyes. Romeo, by Rosaline's high forehead and her scarlet lip, by her fine foot, straight leg, and quivering thigh, and the places that lie near to it, I call for you to appear to us!*

BEN: *If he hears you, you will anger him.*

25   MER: This cannot anger him. 'Twould anger him
         To raise a spirit in his mistress' circle
         Of some strange nature, letting it there stand
         Till she had laid it and conjur'd it down.
         That were some spite; my invocation
30   Is fair and honest: in his mistress' name,
         I conjure only but to raise up him.

         BEN: Come, he hath hid himself among these trees
         To be consorted with the humorous night.
         Blind is his love and best befits the dark.

35   MER: If love be blind, love cannot hit the mark.
         Now will he sit under a medlar tree
         And wish his mistress were that kind of fruit
         As maids call medlars when they laugh alone.
         O, Romeo, that she were, O that she were
40   An open et cetera, thou a pop'rin pear!
         Romeo, good night. I'll to my truckle-bed;
         This field-bed is too cold for me to sleep.
         Come, shall we go?

         BEN: Go then, for 'tis in vain
45   'To seek him here that means not to be found.

                                       [Exeunt.]

MER: *This cannot anger him. It would anger him to raise a spirit in his mistress' presence of some strange nature, letting it stand there until she conjured it down. That would be some spirit; but my spell is fair and honest. In his mistress's name, I conjure only to raise him up.*

BEN: *Come, he has hid himself among these trees to be joined with the humorous night. Since his love is blind, it best fits the darkness.*

MER: *If love is blind, love cannot hit the mark. Now he will sit under a medlar tree and wish his mistress were that kind of fruit as maids call medlars when they laugh alone. Oh, Romeo, if only she were, an open invitation, and you a pear about to burst! Romeo, good night. I'll go to my day-bed; this field-bed is too cold for me to sleep in. Come, shall we go?*

BEN: *Let us go then, for it is in vain to seek someone here who means not to be found.*
[Exit.]

SCENE II
Capulet's orchard.

[Enter Romeo.]

ROM: He jests at scars that never felt a wound.

[Enter Juliet above at a window.]

But soft! What light through yonder window breaks?
It is the East, and Juliet is the sun!
Arise, fair sun, and kill the envious moon,
5   Who is already sick and pale with grief
That thou her maid art far more fair than she.
Be not her maid, since she is envious.
Her vestal livery is but sick and green,
And none but fools do wear it. Cast it off.
10   It is my lady; O, it is my love!
O that she knew she were!
She speaks, yet she says nothing. What of that?
Her eye discourses; I will answer it.
I am too bold; 'tis not to me she speaks.
15   Two of the fairest stars in all the heaven,
Having some business, do entreat her eyes
To twinkle in their spheres till they return.
What if her eyes were there, they in her head?
The brightness of her cheek would shame those stars
20   As daylight doth a lamp; her eyes in heaven
Would through the airy region stream so bright
That birds would sing and think it were not night.
See how she leans her cheek upon her hand!
O that I were a glove upon that hand,
25   That I might touch that cheek!

JUL: Ay me!

ROM: She speaks.
O, speak again, bright angel! for thou art
As glorious to this night, being o'er my head,
30   As is a winged messenger of heaven

SCENE II
Capulet's orchard.

[Enter Romeo.]

ROM: *He who has never felt a wound can jest at scars.*

[Seeing Juliet enter above on balcony.]

But wait! What light comes through that window? It is the east, and Juliet is the sun! Arise, fair sun, and chase away the envious moon; the moon is already sick and pale with grief that you, her maid, are far more fair than she is. Do not be her maid, since she is envious. Her vestal clothing is but sick and green with jealousy, and only fools do wear it. Cast it off. Yes, yes, it is my lady; oh, it is my love! Oh, if only she knew she was! She speaks, yet she says nothing. What of that? Her eye speaks; I will answer it. [Pause] No, I am too bold; it is not to me she speaks. Two of the fairest stars in all the sky, having some business elsewhere, do ask her eyes to twinkle in their place until they return. What if her eyes were there and the stars were in her head? The brightness of her cheek would make those stars pale as daylight does a lamp; her eyes, if stars in heaven, would stream through that airy region so brightly that birds would sing and think it were day. See how she leans her hand upon her cheek! Oh, I wish I were a glove upon that hand, that I might touch that cheek!

JUL: *Oh, me!*

ROM: *She speaks. Oh, speak again, bright angel! You look as glorious to this night, as a winged angel looks to the white-upturned wondering eyes of mortals that fall back to gaze on him when he rides the lazy-pacing clouds and sails upon the bosom of the air.*

Unto the white-upturned wond'ring eyes
Of mortals that fall back to gaze on him
When he bestrides the lazy-pacing clouds
And sails upon the bosom of the air.

35   JUL: O Romeo, Romeo! wherefore art thou Romeo?
Deny thy father and refuse thy name!
Or, if thou wilt not, be but sworn my love,
And I'll no longer be a Capulet.

ROM: [Aside] Shall I hear more, or shall I speak at this?

40   JUL: 'Tis but thy name that is my enemy.
Thou art thyself, though not a Montague.
What's Montague? it is nor hand, nor foot,
Nor arm, nor face, nor any other part
Belonging to a man. O, be some other name!
45   What's in a name? That which we call a rose
By any other name would smell as sweet.
So Romeo would, were he not Romeo call'd,
Retain that dear perfection which he owes
Without that title. Romeo, doff thy name;
50   And for that name, which is no part of thee,
Take all myself.

ROM: I take thee at thy word.
Call me but love, and I'll be new baptiz'd;
Henceforth I never will be Romeo.

55   JUL: What man art thou that, thus bescreen'd in night,
So stumblest on my counsel?

ROM: By a name
I know not how to tell thee who I am.
My name, dear saint, is hateful to myself,
60   Because it is an enemy to thee.
Had I it written, I would tear the word.

JUL: My ears have yet not drunk a hundred words
Of that tongue's utterance, yet I know the sound.
Art thou not Romeo, and a Montague?

JUL: *Oh, Romeo, Romeo! Why are you Romeo? Deny your father and refuse your name! Or, if you will not, be my sworn love, and I'll no longer be a Capulet.*

ROM: [Aside] *Shall I hear more, or shall I speak now?*

JUL: *It is only your name that is my enemy. You are yourself, regardless of your name. What is a Montague? It is not a hand, not a foot, nor arm, nor face, nor any other part belonging to a man. Oh, be some other name! What's in a name? That which we call a rose by any other name would smell as sweet. So would Romeo, if he were not called Romeo, still retain that dear perfection which he owns without that name. Romeo, drop your name, and exchange that name, which is no part of you, for all of myself.*

ROM: [Speaks aloud.] *I take you at your word. Call me only your love, and I'll be newly baptized; from now on I never will be Romeo.*

JUL: *What man are you that, thus hidden by the night, stumbles on my thoughts?*

ROM: *By a name I know not how to tell you. My name, dear saint, is hateful to myself because it is an enemy to you. Had I written it, I would tear up the word.*

JUL: *My ears have not yet drunk a hundred words of that tongue's utterance, yet I know the sound. Are you not Romeo, and a Montague?*

65   ROM: Neither, fair maid, if either thee dislike.

JUL: How cam'st thou hither, tell me, and wherefore?
The orchard walls are high and hard to climb,
And the place death, considering who thou art,
If any of my kinsmen find thee here.

70   ROM: With love's light wings did I o'erperch these walls;
For stony limits cannot hold love out,
And what love can do, that dares love attempt.
Therefore thy kinsmen are no let to me.

JUL: If they do see thee, they will murder thee.

75   ROM: Alack, there lies more peril in thine eye
Than twenty of their swords! Look thou but sweet,
And I am proof against their enmity.

JUL: I would not for the world they saw thee here.

ROM: I have night's cloak to hide me from their eyes;
80   And but thou love me, let them find me here.
My life were better ended by their hate
Than death prorogued, wanting of thy love.

JUL: By whose direction found'st thou out this place?

ROM: By love, that first did prompt me to inquire.
85   He lent me counsel, and I lent him eyes.
I am no pilot; yet, wert thou as far
As that vast shore wash'd with the farthest sea,
I would adventure for such merchandise.

JUL: Thou knowest the mask of night is on my face;
90   Else would a maiden blush bepaint my cheek
For that which thou hast heard me speak to-night.
Fain would I dwell on form, fain, fain deny
What I have spoke; but farewell complement!
Dost thou love me? I know thou wilt say 'Ay';
95   And I will take thy word. Yet, if thou swear'st,

74

ROM: *Neither, fair maid, if you dislike either of them.*

JUL: *How did you come here? Tell me how and also why. The orchard walls are high and hard to climb, and this place, considering who you are, is death if any of my kinsmen find you here.*

ROM: *With love's light wings I flew over these walls, for stone walls cannot hold love out nor hold out what love can do and dares to attempt. Therefore, your kinsmen are no threat to me.*

JUL: *If they see you, they will murder you.*

ROM: *There is more peril in your eyes than in twenty of their swords! Look sweetly on me, and I will prove that their hatred cannot harm me.*

JUL: *I hope for all the world that they do not see you here.*

ROM: *I have the darkness to hide me from their eyes, and if you love me, let them find me here. It is better that my life were ended by their hate than be prolonged if I lack your love.*

JUL: *By whose direction did you find out this place?*

ROM: *By love's direction, which first prompted me to inquire. He gave me counsel, and I lent him eyes. I am no pilot, yet, were you as far away as a distant shore washed by the farthest sea, I would venture for such merchandise.*

JUL: *You know the mask of night is on my face; otherwise a maiden's blush would paint my cheek for that which you have heard me speak tonight. Gladly would I dwell on form—gladly, gladly deny what I have spoken; but good-bye, etiquette! Do you love me? I know you will say 'Ay,' and I will take you at your word. Yet, if you swear, you may prove false. They say Jove laughs at lovers' lies. Oh, gentle Romeo, if you do love me, pronounce it faithfully. Or if you think I am won too quickly, I'll frown, and be stubborn, and say no*

Thou mayst prove false. At lovers' perjuries,
They say Jove laughs. O gentle Romeo,
If thou dost love, pronounce it faithfully.
Or if thou thinkest I am too quickly won,
100 I'll frown, and be perverse, and say thee nay,
So thou wilt woo; but else, not for the world.
In truth, fair Montague, I am too fond,
And therefore thou mayst think my haviour light;
But trust me, gentleman, I'll prove more true
105 Than those that have more cunning to be strange.
I should have been more strange, I must confess,
But that thou overheard'st, ere I was ware,
My true love's passion. Therefore pardon me,
And not impute this yielding to light love,
110 Which the dark night hath so discovered.

ROM: Lady, by yonder blessed moon I swear,
 That tips with silver all these fruit-tree tops—

JUL: O, swear not by the moon, the inconstant moon,
 That monthly changes in her circled orb,
115 Lest that thy love prove likewise variable.

ROM: What shall I swear by?

JUL: Do not swear at all;
 Or if thou wilt, swear by thy gracious self,
 Which is the god of my idolatry,
120 And I'll believe thee.

ROM: If my heart's dear love—

JUL: Well, do not swear. Although I joy in thee,
 I have no joy of this contract to-night.
 It is too rash, too unadvis'd, too sudden;
125 Too like the lightning, which doth cease to be
 Ere one can say 'It lightens.' Sweet, good night!
 This bud of love, by summer's ripening breath,
 May prove a beauteous flower when next we meet.
 Good night, good night! As sweet repose and rest
130 Come to thy heart as that within my breast!

76

to you so you will woo; but otherwise I would, not for the world. In truth, fair Montague, I am too fond, and, therefore, you may think my behavior light, but trust me, gentleman: I'll prove more true than those that have more cunning to be distant. I should have hidden my feelings more, I must confess. You over-heard my true-love passion before I was aware. Therefore, pardon me, but do not take my manner which you so discovered this dark night for casual love.

Rom: *Lady, by yonder blessed moon, which tips with silver all these fruit-tree tops, I swear—*

Jul: *Oh, swear not by the moon, the inconstant moon, which changes monthly in her circled orbit, unless your love proves likewise variable.*

Rom: *What shall I swear by?*

Jul: *Do not swear at all, or if you will, swear on your gracious self, which is the god of my worship, and I'll believe you.*

Rom: *If my heart's dear love—*

Jul: *Well, do not swear. Although I am happy with you, I have no joy in this contract tonight. It is too rash, too ill-advised, too sudden, too like the light-ning, which ceases to be almost before one can say, "It lightens." Sweet, good night! This bud of love , by summer's ripening breath, may prove a beauteous flower when we meet next. Good night, good night! May as sweet a repose and rest come to your heart as I have within my breast!*

ROM: O, wilt thou leave me so unsatisfied?

JUL: What satisfaction canst thou have to-night?

ROM: Th' exchange of thy love's faithful vow for mine.

JUL: I gave thee mine before thou didst request it;
135   And yet I would it were to give again.

ROM: Would'st thou withdraw it? For what purpose, love?

JUL: But to be frank, and give it thee again.
        And yet I wish but for the thing I have.
        My bounty is as boundless as the sea,
140   My love as deep; the more I give to thee,
        The more I have, for both are infinite.
        I hear some noise within. Dear love, adieu! *[Nurse calls within.]*
        Anon, good Nurse! Sweet Montague, be true.
        Stay but a little, I will come again.   *[Exit.]*

145   ROM: O blessed, blessed night! I am afeard,
        Being in night, all this is but a dream,
        Too flattering-sweet to be substantial.

[Enter Juliet above.]

      JUL: Three words, dear Romeo, and good night indeed.
        If that thy bent of love be honourable,
150   Thy purpose marriage, send me word to-morrow,
        By one that I'll procure to come to thee,
        Where and what time thou wilt perform the rite;
        And all my fortunes at thy foot I'll lay
        And follow thee my lord throughout the world.

155   NURSE: *[Within.]* Madam!

      JUL: I come, anon.—But if thou meanest not well,
        I do beseech thee—

      NURSE: *[Within.]* Madam!

ROM: *Oh, will you leave me so unsatisfied?*

JUL: *What satisfaction can you have tonight?*

ROM: *The exchange of your love's faithful vow for mine.*

JUL: *I gave you mine before you did request it, and yet I wish it were still there to give again.*

ROM: *Would you withdraw your statement of love? For what purpose, love?*

JUL: *Only to be generous and give it to you again. And yet I wish only for the thing I have. My bounty is as boundless as the sea, my love is as deep; the more I give to you, the more I have, for both are infinite. I hear some noise within. Dear love, good-bye!* [Nurse calls within.]
Right away, good Nurse! Sweet Montague, be true. Remain here only a little; I will come back. [Exit.]

ROM: *Oh blessed, blessed night! I am afraid that, because this is night, all this is only a dream, too good to be true.*

[Enter Juliet above.]

JUL: *Three words, dear Romeo, and then good night indeed. If your idea of love is honorable and your purpose is marriage, send me word tomorrow through someone I'll arrange to come to you. Tell the messenger where and at what time you will perform the ceremony, and I'll lay all my fortunes at your feet and follow you, my lord, throughout the world.*

NURSE: [Within.] *Madam!*

JUL: *I come, right away—But if you do not mean to do well, I do ask you—*

NURSE: [Within.] *Madam!*

JUL: By-and-by, I come.—
160   To cease thy suit and leave me to my grief.
         To-morrow will I send.

ROM: So thrive my soul—

JUL: A thousand times good night!   *[Exit.]*

ROM: A thousand times the worse, to want thy light!
165   Love goes toward love as schoolboys from their books;
         But love from love, towards school with heavy looks.

[Enter Juliet again, above.]

JUL: Hist! Romeo, hist! O for a falconer's voice
         To lure this tassel-gentle back again!
         Bondage is hoarse and may not speak aloud;
170   Else would I tear the cave where Echo lies,
         And make her airy tongue more hoarse than mine
         With repetition of my Romeo's name.
         Romeo!

ROM: It is my soul that calls upon my name.
175   How silver-sweet sound lovers' tongues by night,
         Like softest music to attending ears!

JUL: Romeo!

ROM: My dear?

JUL: What o'clock to-morrow
180   Shall I send to thee?

ROM: By the hour of nine.

JUL: I will not fail. 'Tis twenty years till then.
         I have forgot why I did call thee back.

ROM: Let me stand here till thou remember it.

JUL: I'll come soon—to stop your actions and leave me to my grief. I will send someone tomorrow.

ROM: My soul does thrive—

JUL: A thousand times good night!   [Exit.]

ROM: It is a thousand times the worse to lack your light! Love goes toward love as happy schoolboys move away from their books, but love goes away from love with the sad looks of boys going to school.

[Enter Juliet again, above.]

JUL: Listen! Romeo, hear! Oh, for a falconer's voice to lure this beautiful bird, Romeo, back again! Being trapped here, I may not speak aloud. Otherwise, I would tear at the cave where Echo lies and make Echo's airy tongue more hoarse with shouting than mine, with repetition of my Romeo's name. Romeo!

ROM: It is my soul, my love, that calls my name. Like silver-belled lovers' tongues by night, like softest music to eager-listening ears!

JUL: Romeo!

ROM: My dear?

JUL: At what time tomorrow shall I send a messenger to you?

ROM: By the hour of nine.

JUL: I will not fail. It will seem like twenty years until then. I have forgotten why I called you back.

ROM: Let me stand here until you remember it.

185   JUL: I shall forget, to have thee still stand there,
        Remembering how I love thy company.

      ROM: And I'll still stay, to have thee still forget,
        Forgetting any other home but this.

      JUL: 'Tis almost morning. I would have thee gone—
190   And yet no farther than a wanton's bird,
        That lets it hop a little from her hand,
        Like a poor prisoner in his twisted gyves,
        And with a silk thread plucks it back again,
        So loving-jealous of his liberty.

195   ROM: I would I were thy bird.

      JUL: Sweet, so would I.
        Yet I should kill thee with much cherishing.
        Good night, good night! Parting is such sweet sorrow,
        That I shall say good night till it be morrow.   *[Exit.]*

200   ROM: Sleep dwell upon thine eyes, peace in thy breast!
        Would I were sleep and peace, so sweet to rest!
        Hence will I to my ghostly father's cell,
        His help to crave and my dear hap to tell.   *[Exit]*

JUL: I shall forget and leave you standing there, remembering how I love your company.

ROM: And I'll still stay in order to have you still forget, and I'll forget any other home but this.

JUL: It is almost morning. I wish you were gone—but no farther than someone's pet would go, who lets it hop a little from her hand, like a poor prisoner in his twisted chains, and with a silk thread plucks it back again, so loving, yet so jealous of its liberty.

ROM: I wish I were your bird.

JUL: Sweet, so do I. Yet I should kill you with too much cherishing. Good night, good night! Parting is such sweet sorrow, that until tomorrow I shall keep on saying good night. [Exit.]

ROM: Sleep dwell upon your eyes and peace in your heart! I wish I were sleep and peace; it would be sweet to rest there! I will go to Friar Laurence's cell to ask for his help and to tell him my dear story. [Exit.]

SCENE III
Friar Laurence's cell.

[Enter Friar Laurence alone, with a basket.]

FRIAR: The grey-ey'd morn smiles on the frowning night,
Check'ring the Eastern clouds with streaks of light;
And flecked darkness like a drunkard reels
From forth day's path and Titan's fiery wheels.
5   Now, ere the sun advance his burning eye
The day to cheer and night's dank dew to dry,
I must up-fill this osier cage of ours
With baleful weeds and precious-juiced flowers.
The earth that's nature's mother is her tomb.
10   What is her burying grave, that is her womb;
And from her womb children of divers kind
We sucking on her natural bosom find;
Many for many virtues excellent,
None but for some, and yet all different.
15   O, mickle is the powerful grace that lies
In plants, herbs, stones, and their true qualities;
For naught so vile that on the earth doth live
But to the earth some special good doth give;
Nor aught so good but, strain'd from that fair use,
20   Revolts from true birth, stumbling on abuse.
Virtue itself turns vice, being misapplied,
And vice sometime's by action dignified.
Within the infant rind of this small flower
Poison hath residence, and medicine power;
25   For this, being smelt, with that part cheers each part;
Being tasted, slays all senses with the heart.
Two such opposed kings encamp them still
In man as well as herbs—grace and rude will;
And where the worser is predominant,
30   Full soon the canker death eats up that plant.

[Enter Romeo.]

ROM: Good morrow, father.

84

SCENE III

Friar Laurence's cell.

[Enter Friar Laurence alone, with a basket.]

FRIAR: *The grey-eyed morning smiles on the frowning night, speckling the eastern clouds with streaks of light, and darkness staggers away like a drunkard from the day's path and Titan's fiery wheels. Now, before the sun advances, and his burning eye cheers the day and dries night's wet dew to dryness, I must fill up this willow basket with harmful weeds and precious-juiced flowers. Earth is both the mother and the tomb of nature. Life comes from her burial mounds, and from her womb, children of various kinds come to suck on her natural bosom. Many have many excellent virtues; no one is without some, and yet all are different. Great is the powerful grace that lies in plants, herbs, stones, and their true qualities, for nothing is so vile that lives on the earth that it does not give to the earth some special good: Similarly, nothing is so good that, twisted from its intended use, will not revolt from its true purpose and cause an evil. Virtue itself can turn vice, being misapplied; and vice, sometimes, by action can be beneficial. Within the small rind of this small flower, both poison and medicinal power reside. This flower, when smelled, cheers all the senses, but when tasted, can slay all senses and the heart. Two such opposing forces exist in men as well as herbs—that is, both good and evil—and where the evil dominates, soon the worm, death, eats up that plant.*

[Enter Romeo.]

ROM: *Good morning, father.*

FRIAR: Benedicite!
    What early tongue so sweet saluteth me?
    Young son, it argues a distempered head
35   So soon to bid good morrow to thy bed.
    Care keeps his watch in every old man's eye,
    And where care lodges sleep will never lie;
    But where unbruised youth with unstuff'd brain
    Doth couch his limbs, there golden sleep doth reign.
40   Therefore thy earliness doth me assure
    Thou art uprous'd with some distemp'rature;
    Or if not so, then here I hit it right—
    Our Romeo hath not been in bed to-night.

ROM: That last is true—the sweeter rest was mine.

45 FRIAR: God pardon sin! Wast thou with Rosaline?

ROM: With Rosaline, my ghostly father? No.
    I have forgot that name, and that name's woe.

FRIAR: That's my good son! But where hast thou been then?

ROM: I'll tell thee ere thou ask it me again.
50   I have been feasting with mine enemy,
    Where on a sudden one hath wounded me
    That's by me wounded. Both our remedies
    Within thy help and holy physic lies.
    I bear no hatred, blessed man, for, lo,
55   My intercession likewise steads my foe.

FRIAR: Be plain, good son, and homely in thy drift
    Riddling confession finds but riddling shrift.

ROM: Then plainly know my heart's dear love is set
    On the fair daughter of rich Capulet;
60   As mine on hers, so hers is set on mine,
    And all combin'd, save what thou must combine
    By holy marriage. When, and where, and how
    We met, we woo'd, and made exchange of vow,
    I'll tell thee as we pass; but this I pray,
65   That thou consent to marry us to-day.

FRIAR: *Bless you! What tongue sweetly salutes me so early? Young son, it reveals a worried mind to rise so early from your bed. Care keeps his watch in every old man's eye, and where care lodges, sleep will never lie. Where a fresh youth with a clear head rests his limbs, however, golden sleep reigns. Therefore, your earliness does convince me that you are kept awake by some problem, or if not, then here I am accurate—our Romeo has not been to bed tonight.*

ROM: *That last is true—the sweeter rest was mine indeed.*

FRIAR: *God pardon sin! Were you with Rosaline?*

ROM: *With Rosaline, my ghostly father? No. I have forgotten that name and that name's suffering.*

FRIAR: *That is good, my son! But where have you been?*

ROM: *I'll tell you before you ask me again. I have been feasting with my enemy, when all of a sudden, a woman wounded me and was wounded by me. Our remedies lie within your help and holy practice. I bear no hatred, blessed man, for my request helps my foe as well as me.*

FRIAR: *Be plain, good son, and be plain in telling your story. A confusing confession finds only riddling forgiveness.*

ROM: *Then, plainly know that my heart's dear love is set on the fair daughter of rich Capulet. As mine is on hers, so hers is set on mine; we are combined, except what you must join by holy marriage. When, where, and how we met, wooed, and exchanged promises, I'll tell you as we talk; but this I ask: that you consent to marry us today.*

FRIAR: Holy Saint Francis! What a change is here!
Is Rosaline, that thou didst love so dear,
So soon forsaken? Young men's love then lies
Not truly in their hearts, but in their eyes.
70   Jesu Maria! What a deal of brine
Hath wash'd thy sallow cheeks for Rosaline!
How much salt water thrown away in waste,
To season love, that of it doth not taste!
The sun not yet thy sighs from heaven clears,
75   Thy old groans ring yet in mine ancient ears.
Lo, here upon thy cheek the stain doth sit
Of an old tear that is not wash'd off yet.
If e'er thou wast thyself, and these woes thine,
Thou and these woes were all for Rosaline.
80   And art thou chang'd? Pronounce this sentence then:
Women may fall when there's no strength in men.

ROM: Thou chid'st me oft for loving Rosaline.

FRIAR: For doting, not for loving, pupil mine.

ROM: And bad'st me bury love.

85   FRIAR: Not in a grave
To lay one in, another out to have.

ROM: I pray thee chide not. She whom I love now
Doth grace for grace and love for love allow.
The other did not so.

90   FRIAR: O, she knew well
Thy love did read by rote, and could not spell.
But come, young waverer, come go with me.
In one respect I'll thy assistant be;
For this alliance may so happy prove
95   To turn your households' rancour to pure love.

ROM: O, let us hence! I stand on sudden haste.

FRIAR: Wisely, and slow. They stumble that run fast.   *[Exeunt.]*

FRIAR: *Holy Saint Francis! What a change is here! Is Rosaline, that you did love so dearly, so soon forsaken? If so, young men's love does not lie in their hearts, but in their eyes. Jesus Mary! What a lot of tears have washed your pale cheeks for Rosaline! How much salt water was wasted and thrown away to season a love it does not even taste! The sun has not yet cleared your sighs from heaven; your old groans ring yet in my old ears. Look, here upon your cheek the stain sits of an old tear that is not yet washed off. If ever you were yourself and these woes yours, you and these woes were always for Rosaline. And are you changed? Then pronounce this sentence: it is no wonder women fall, when there's no strength in men.*

ROM: *You scolded me for loving Rosaline.*

FRIAR: *For being so passionate, not for loving, my pupil.*

ROM: *And you told me to bury my love.*

FRIAR: *Not to lay one romance in a grave, and take out another.*

ROM: *Please do not scold me. She whom I love now, returns my favor and my love. The other did not do so.*

FRIAR: *She knew well that you loved only by memorization and not by true understanding. But come, young waverer, come with me. In one respect I'll be your assistant, for this marriage may happily turn your households' hatred into pure love.*

ROM: *Let us go! I am so impatient!*

FRIAR: *Wisely, and slow. Those who run fast stumble.*   [Exit.]

89

SCENE IV
A Street.

[Enter Benvolio and Mercutio.]

MER: Where the devil should this Romeo be?
Came he not home to-night?

BEN: Not to his father's. I spoke with his man.

MER: Why, that same pale hard-hearted wench,
5   that Rosaline, torments him so that he will sure run mad.

BEN: Tybalt, the kinsman to old Capulet,
Hath sent a letter to his father's house.

MER: A challenge, on my life.

BEN: Romeo will answer it.

10   MER: Any man that can write may answer a letter.

BEN: Nay, he will answer the letter's master, how he dares, being dared.

MER: Alas, poor Romeo, he is already dead! stabb'd with a white
wench's black eye; shot through the ear with a love song; the very
pin of his heart cleft with the blind bow-boy's butt-shaft; and is he
15   a man to encounter Tybalt?

BEN: Why, what is Tybalt?

MER: More than Prince of Cats, I can tell you. O, he's the courageous
captain of compliments. He fights as you sing pricksong, keeps
time, distance, and proportion; rests me his minim rest, one, two,
20   and the third in your bosom! the very butcher of a silk button, a
duellist, a duellist! a gentle man of the very first house, of the
firstand second cause. Ah, the immortal passado! the punto
reverse! the ha!

SCENE IV

A Street.

[Enter Benvolio and Mercutio.]

MER: Where the devil can this Romeo be? Did he not come home last night?

BEN: Not to his father's. I spoke with his servant.

MER: Why, that same pale hard-hearted wench, that Rosaline, torments him so that he will surely become mad.

BEN: Tybalt, the kinsman to old Capulet, has sent a letter to his father's house.

MER: A challenge, I do believe.

BEN: Romeo will answer it.

MER: Any man that can write may answer a letter.

BEN: No, he will answer Tybalt, not Tybalt's letter because he has been challenged.

MER: Alas, poor Romeo, he is already dead! Stabbed with a white wench's dark eye, shot through the ear with a love song, the very center of his heart split with blind Cupid's arrow. Is such a man to confront Tybalt?

BEN: Why, what is Tybalt?

MER: More than the Prince of Cats, I can tell you. Oh, he's the courageous captain of our time. He fights as you sing printed songs—he keeps time, distance, and proportion, rests only short rests: one, two, and the third in your bosom! The very butcher of a silk button—a duelist, a duelist! A swordsman of first quality when there is just cause. Ah, the immortal forehand! The backhand reverse! The kill!

BEN: The what?

25 MER: The pox of such antic, lisping, affecting fantasticoes—these new
tuners of accent! 'By Jesu, a very good blade! a very tall man! a
very good whore!' Why, is not this a lamentable thing, grandsir,
that we should be thus af-flicted with these strange flies, these
fashion-mongers, these pardona-mi's, who stand so much on the
30 new form that they cannot sit at ease on the old bench? O, their
bones, their bones!

[Enter Romeo.]

BEN: Here comes Romeo! here comes Romeo!

MER: Without his roe, like a dried herring. O flesh, flesh, how art thou
fishified! Now is he for the numbers that Petrarch flowed in.
35 Laura, to his lady, was but a kitchen wench (marry, she had a
better love to berhyme her), Dido a dowdy, Cleopatra a gypsy,
Helen and Hero hildings and harlots, Thisbe a gray eye or so, but
not to the purpose. Signior Romeo, bon jour! There's a French
salutation to your French slop. You gave us the counterfeit fairly
40 last night.

ROM: Good morrow to you both. What counterfeit did I give you?

MER: The slip, sir, the slip. Can you not conceive?

ROM: Pardon, good Mercutio. My business was great, and in such a
case as mine a man may strain courtesy.

45 MER: That's as much as to say, such a case as yours constrains a man
to bow in the hams.

ROM: Meaning, to curtsy.

MER: Thou hast most kindly hit it.

ROM: A most courteous exposition.

50 MER: Nay, I am the very pink of courtesy.

BEN: *The what?*

MER: *Curse such antics, effeminate braggarts—you new tellers of tales! "By Jesus, a very good blade! A very tall man! A very good whore!" Why, is not this a lamentable thing, grandsir, that we should be thus afflicted with these strange flies, these flashy dressers, these "pardona-mi's," which stand so much on new ceremonies that they cannot sit at ease on the old ones? Oh, their bones, their bones!*

[Enter Romeo.]

BEN: *Here comes Romeo! Here comes Romeo!*

MER: *Without his "Roe," like a dried herring. Oh, flesh, flesh, how fishy you are! Now Romeo will write verses like Petrarch wrote Laura, his lady, who was only a common girl (yet she had a better love to rhyme her). Dido is plain, Cleopatra is a gypsy, Helen and Hero are unworthy and easy, and Thisbe, though she has gray eyes, is not in the running. Signior Romeo, good day! There's a French welcome to your French clothes. You played false with us last night.*

ROM: *Good morning to you both. What falsehood did I give to you?*

MER: *The slip, sir, you gave us the slip. Do you not understand?*

ROM: *Pardon me, dear Mercutio. My business was great, and in such a case as mine, a man may strain friendship.*

MER: *That's as much as to say that in a case such as yours, a man may bow his knees.*

ROM: *Meaning to curtsy.*

MER: *You have most truly hit upon it.*

ROM: *A most courteous speech.*

MER: *No, I am the very pink of courtesy.*

Rom: Pink for flower.

Mer: Right.

Rom: Why, then is my pump well-flower'd.

Mer: Well said! Follow me this jest now till thou hast worn out thy
55   pump, that, when the single sole of it is worn, the jest may remain,
after the wearing, solely singular.

Rom: O single-sold jest, solely singular for the singleness!

Mer: Come between us, good Benvolio! My wits faint.

Rom: Switch and spurs, switch and spurs! or I'll cry a match.

60   Mer: Nay, if our wits run the wild-goose chase, I am done; for thou
hast more of the wild goose in one of thy wits than, I am sure, I
have in my whole five. Was I with you there for the goose?

Rom: Thou wast never with me for anything when thou wast not
there for the goose.

65   Mer: I will bite thee by the ear for that jest.

Rom: Nay, good goose, bite not!

Mer: Thy wit is a very bitter sweeting; it is a most sharp sauce.

Rom: And is it not, then, well serv'd in to a sweet goose?

Mer: O, here's a wit of cheverel, that stretches from an inch narrow to
70   an ell broad!

Rom: I stretch it out for that word 'broad,' which, added to the goose,
proves thee far and wide a broad goose.

Mer: Why, is not this better now than groaning for love? Now art thou
sociable, now art thou Romeo; now art thou what thou art, by art
75   as well as by nature. For this drivelling love is like a great natural
that runs lolling up and down to hide his bauble in a hole.

94

ROM: "Pink" meaning flower.

MER: Right.

ROM: Why, then my shoe is well-flowered too.

MER: Well said! I will follow this jest now until you have worn out your shoe, so, when the single sole of it is worn out, your jest will remain, solely alone.

ROM: Oh, a weak joke. In a class by itself but only because it is so stupid!

MER: Come between us, good Benvolio! My wits faint at this cleverness.

ROM: Keep going! More! More, or I'll cry that I've won the match.

MER: No, if our wits run the wild-goose chase, I am done, for you have more of the wild goose in one of your wits than, I am sure, I have in my whole five. Have I cooked your goose?

ROM: You never kept up with me for anything except when you played the silly goose.

MER: I will bite you on the ear for that jest.

ROM: No, good goose, don't bite me!

MER: Your wit is a very bitter sweet; it is a sharp sauce.

ROM: And is it not well served to a sweet goose?

MER: Oh, here's a wit of leather that stretches from a narrow inch to a broad piece!

ROM: I stretch it out for that word "broad," which, added to the goose, proves you far and wide to be a large goose.

MER: Why, is this not better than groaning for love? Now you are sociable; now you are Romeo; now you are what you are, by art as well as by nature. For silly love is like a great fool that runs up and down and then hides his stick in a hole.

BEN: Stop there, stop there!

MER: Thou desirest me to stop in my tale against the hair.

BEN: Thou wouldst else have made thy tale large.

80   MER: O, thou art deceiv'd! I would have made it short; for I was come
       to the whole depth of my tale, and meant indeed to occupy the
       argument no longer.

ROM: Here's goodly gear!

[Enter Nurse and her Man, Peter.]

MER: A sail, a sail!

85   BEN: Two, two! a shirt and a smock.

NURSE: Peter!

PETER: Anon.

NURSE: My fan, Peter.

MER: Good Peter, to hide her face; for her fan's the fairer face of the
90   two.

NURSE: God ye good morrow, gentlemen.

MER: God ye good-den, fair gentlewoman.

NURSE: Is it good-den?

MER: 'Tis no less, I tell ye; for the bawdy hand of the dial is now upon
95   the prick of noon.

NURSE: Out upon you! What a man are you!

ROM: One, gentlewoman, that God hath made for himself to mar.

BEN: *Stop there; stop there!*

MER: *You desire me to stop short in my tale.*

BEN: *You would have made your tale too large.*

MER: *Oh, you are deceived! I would have made it short, for I was coming to the whole depth of my tale, and I meant indeed to follow the argument no longer.*

ROM: *Here is some goodly baggage!*

[Enter Nurse and her servant, Peter.]

MER: *A sail, a sail!*

BEN: *Two, two! A shirt and a smock.*

NURSE: *Peter!*

PETER: *Yes.*

NURSE: *My fan, Peter.*

MER: *Good Peter, use the fan to hide her face, for her fan's the fairer face of the two.*

NURSE: *Good morning to you, gentlemen.*

MER: *Good afternoon to you, fair gentlewoman.*

NURSE: *Is it afternoon already?*

MER: *Yes, it is, I tell you; for the bawdy hand of the sundial now says noon.*

NURSE: *Well, now! What kind of man are you?*

ROM: *One, gentlewoman, that God has made for himself to mar.*

NURSE: By my troth, it is well said. 'For himself to mar,' quoth a?
    Gentlemen, can any of you tell me where I may find the young
100   Romeo?

ROM: I can tell you; but young Romeo will be older when you have
    found him than he was when you sought him. I am the youngest
    of that name, for fault of a worse.

NURSE: You say well.

105   MER: Yea, is the worst well? Very well took, i' faith! wisely, wisely.

NURSE: If you be he, sir, I desire some confidence with you.

BEN: She will indite him to some supper.

MER: A bawd, a bawd, a bawd! So ho!

ROM: What hast thou found?

110   MER: No hare, sir; unless a hare, sir, in a lenten pie, that is something
    stale and hoar ere it be spent.
    [He walks by them and sings.]
        An old hare hoar,
        And an old hare hoar,
        Is very good meat in Lent;
115   But a hare that is hoar
        Is too much for a score
        When it hoars ere it be spent.
    Romeo, will you come to your father's? We'll to dinner thither.

ROM: I will follow you.

120   MER: Farewell, ancient Lady. Farewell,
    [Sings] lady, lady, lady.   *[Exeunt Mercutio, Benvolio.]*

NURSE: Marry, farewell! I pray you, sir, what saucy
    merchant was this that was so full of his ropery?

NURSE: *By my faith, it is well said. "For himself to mar," says he? Gentlemen, can any of you tell me where I may find the young Romeo?*

ROM: *I can tell you, but young Romeo will be older when you have found him than he was when you sought him. I am, for lack of a better name, the youngest of that name.*

NURSE: *You speak well.*

MER: *Yes, but is the worst well? Very well taken, in faith! Wisely, wisely.*

NURSE: *If you be he, sir, I desire a conference with you.*

BEN: *She will invite him to some supper.*

MER: *A bawdy woman! Aha!*

ROM: *What have you found?*

MER: *No hare, sir, unless a hare, sir, in a meatless pie that becomes something stale and moldy before it is used up.*
[Mercutio walks by them and sings.]
>   *An old hairy whore*
>   *And an old hoary hare*
>   *Are fine to have during lent*
>   *But a hare that is rotten*
>   *Is to much to be gotten*
>   *When it dies for what was spent.*
Romeo, will you go to your father's? If so, we'll go to dinner there.

ROM: *I will follow you.*

MER: *Farewell, ancient lady. Farewell,*
    [Sings] *lady, lady, lady.*   [Exit Mercutio, Benvolio.]

NURSE: *Well, farewell! I ask you, sir, what saucy merchant was this who was so full of his foolishness?*

ROM: A gentleman, Nurse, that loves to hear himself talk and will
125   speak more in a minute than he will stand to in a month.

NURSE: An 'a speak anything against me, I'll take him down, an 'a were
lustier than he is, and twenty such jacks; and if I cannot, I'll find
those that shall. Scurvy knave! I am none of his flirt-gills; I am
none of his skains-mates. And thou must stand by too, and suffer
130   every knave to use me at his pleasure!

PETER: I saw no man use you at his pleasure. If I had, my weapon
should quickly have been out, I warrant you. I dare draw as soon
as another man, if I see occasion in a good quarrel, and the law on
my side.

135   NURSE: Now, afore God, I am so vexed that every part about me
quivers. Scurvy knave! Pray you, sir, a word; and, as I told you, my
young lady bid me enquire you out. What she bid me say, I will
keep to myself; but first let me tell ye, if ye should lead her into a
fool's paradise, as they say, it were a very gross kind of behaviour,
140   as they say; for the gentle woman is young; and therefore, if you
should deal double with her, truly it were an ill thing to be off'red
to any gentlewoman, and very weak dealing.

ROM: Nurse, commend me to thy lady and mistress. I protest unto
thee—

145   NURSE: Good heart, and i' faith I will tell her as much. Lord, Lord! she
will be a joyful woman.

ROM: What wilt thou tell her, Nurse? Thou dost not mark me.

NURSE: I will tell her, sir, that you do protest, which, as I take it, is a
gentlemanlike offer.

150   ROM: Bid her devise some means to come to shrift
This afternoon;
And there she shall at Friar Laurence' cell
Be shriv'd and married. Here is for thy pains.

NURSE: No, truly, sir; not a penny.

ROM: *A gentleman, Nurse, that loves to hear himself talk and will speak more in a minute than he will accept responsibility for in a month.*

NURSE: *If he speaks anything against me, I'll knock him down, even if he were lustier than he is and there were twenty such fools, and if I could not, I'd find those who could. He is a nasty boy! I am not one of his loose women; I am not one of his cutthroats. [To Peter.] And you stand idly by, too, and let every knave abuse me for his pleasure!*

PETER: *I saw no man abuse you for his pleasure. If I had, my weapon should quickly have been out, I promise you. I dare draw as soon as another man if I see reason in a good quarrel, and the law is on my side.*

NURSE: *Now, before God, I am so upset that every part about me quivers. That nasty fool! I beg you, sir, a word; and, as I told you, my young lady bids me inquire about you. What she bids me say, I will keep to myself, but first let me tell you, if you should lead her into a fool's paradise, as they say, it would be a very gross kind of behavior, as they say, for the gentlewoman is young. Therefore, if you should mislead and use her, truly it would be a bad thing to be offered to any gentlewoman and a very poor deal.*

ROM: *Nurse, remember me to your lady and mistress. I protest to you—*

NURSE: *A good heart, and I believe I will tell her as much. Lord, Lord! She will be a joyful woman.*

ROM: *What can you tell her, Nurse? You do not pay much attention to me.*

NURSE: *I will tell her, sir, that you do affirm your feelings which, as I take it, are gentlemanlike offers.*

ROM: *Bid her devise some means to come to confession this afternoon, and while at Friar Laurence's cell, she shall be confessed and married. Here is something for your trouble.*

NURSE: *No, truly, sir, not a penny.*

155   ROM: Go to! I say you shall.

NURSE: This afternoon, sir? Well, she shall be there.

ROM: And stay, good Nurse, behind the abbey wall.
        Within this hour my man shall be with thee
        And bring thee cords made like a tackled stair,
160   Which to the high topgallant of my joy
        Must be my convoy in the secret night.
        Farewell. Be trusty, and I'll quit thy pains.
        Farewell. Commend me to thy mistress.

NURSE: Now God in heaven bless thee! Hark you, sir.

165   ROM: What say'st thou, my dear Nurse?

NURSE: Is your man secret? Did you ne'er hear say,
        Two may keep counsel, putting one away?

ROM: I warrant thee my man's as true as steel.

NURSE: Well, sir, my mistress is the sweetest lady. Lord, Lord! when
170   'twas a little prating thing—O, there is a nobleman in town, one
        Paris, that would fain lay knife aboard; but she, good soul, had as
        lieve see a toad, a very toad, as see him. I anger her sometimes, and
        tell her that Paris is the properer man; but I'll warrant you, when
        I say so, she looks as pale as any clout in the versal world. Doth
175   not rosemary and Romeo begin both with a letter?

ROM: Ay, Nurse; what of that? Both with an R.

NURSE: Ah, mocker! that's the dog's name. R is for the— No; I know
        it begins with some other letter; and she hath the prettiest
        sententious of it, of you and rosemary, that it would do you good
180   to hear it.

ROM: Commend me to thy lady.

NURSE: Ay, a thousand times. *[Exit Romeo.]* Peter!

ROM: *Stop it! I say you shall take this.*

NURSE: *This afternoon, sir? Well, she shall be there.*

ROM: *And, good Nurse, stay behind the abbey's wall. Within this hour, my man shall be with you and bring you cords made like a rope ladder, which will be my means of reaching, in the secret night, the highest mast of my joy. Farewell. Be trustworthy, and I'll reward your trouble. Farewell. Commend me to your mistress.*

NURSE: *Now, God in heaven, bless you! Listen, sir.*

ROM: *What do you say, my dear Nurse?*

NURSE: *Is your man trustworthy? Did you never hear the saying that two may keep a secret if one of them is absent?*

ROM: *I tell you that my man is as true as steel.*

NURSE: *Well, sir, my mistress is the sweetest lady. Lord, Lord! When she was a little babbling thing—Oh, there is a nobleman in town, one Paris, that would love to possess her, but she, good soul, would just as soon see a toad, a very toad, as see him. I anger her sometimes and tell her that Paris is the more handsome man, but I'll grant you, when I say so, she looks as pale as any cloth in the wide world. Do not rosemary and Romeo both begin with the same letter?*

ROM: *Ay, Nurse; what of that? Both with an R.*

NURSE: *Ah, mocker! That's the dog's name. R is for the—no, I know it begins with some other letter. She has the prettiest sentences for it, of you and rosemary; it would do you good to hear it.*

ROM: *Commend me to your lady.*

NURSE: *Ay, a thousand times. [Exit Romeo.] Peter!*

103

PETER: Anon.

NURSE: Peter, take my fan, and go before, and apace.

[Exeunt.]

SCENE V
Capulet's orchard.

[Enter Juliet.]

JUL: The clock struck nine when I did send the Nurse;
   In half an hour she promis'd to return.
   Perchance she cannot meet him. That's not so.
   O, she is lame! Love's heralds should be thoughts,
5 Which ten times faster glide than the sun's beams
   Driving back shadows over low'ring hills.
   Therefore do nimble-pinion'd doves draw Love,
   And therefore hath the wind-swift Cupid wings.
   Now is the sun upon the highmost hill
10 Of this day's journey, and from nine till twelve
   Is three long hours; yet she is not come.
   Had she affections and warm youthful blood,
   She would be as swift in motion as a ball;
   My words would bandy her to my sweet love,
15 And his to me,
   But old folks, many feign as they were dead—
   Unwieldy, slow, heavy and pale as lead.

[Enter Nurse and Peter.]
   O God, she comes! O honey Nurse, what news?
   Hast thou met with him? Send thy man away.

20 NURSE: Peter, stay at the gate.   [Exit Peter.]

JUL: Now, good sweet Nurse—O Lord, why look'stthou sad?
   Though news be sad, yet tell them merrily;
   If good, thou shamest the music of sweet news
   By playing it to me with so sour a face.

PETER: *Here.*

NURSE: *Peter, take my fan and go, and quickly, too.*   [Exit.]

SCENE V

Capulet's orchard.

[Enter Juliet.]

JUL: *The clock struck nine when I did send the Nurse; in half an hour, she promised to return. Maybe she cannot meet him. That's not so. Oh, she is lame! Love's messengers should be thoughts, which glide ten times faster than a sunbeam driving back shadows over distant hills. That's why nimble-winged doves draw Love's chariot and swift Cupid has wings. Now, the sun is upon the highest hill of this day's journey, and from nine till twelve is three long hours; yet she has not come. If she had affections and warm youthful blood, she would be as swift in motion as a ball; my words would toss her towards my sweet love, and his to me. But many old folks move as if they were dead, clumsy, slow, heavy, and pale as lead.*

|Enter Nurse and Peter.]

Oh, God, she comes! Oh, sweetest Nurse, what news? Have you met with him? Send your man away.

NURSE: *Peter, stay at the gate.*   [Exit Peter.]

JUL: *Now, good sweet Nurse—Oh, Lord, why do you look sad? Even though news is sad, tell it merrily. If it is good news, you are shaming the music of sweet news by playing it to me with so sour a face.*

25   NURSE: I am aweary, give me leave awhile.
        Fie, how my bones ache! What a jaunt have I had!

        JUL: I would thou hadst my bones, and I thy news.
        Nay, come, I pray thee speak. Good, good Nurse, speak.

        NURSE: Jesu, what haste! Can you not stay awhile?
30   Do you not see that I am out of breath?

        JUL: How art thou out of breath when thou hast breath
        To say to me that thou art out of breath?
        The excuse that thou dost make in this delay
        Is longer than the tale thou dost excuse.
35   Is thy news good or bad? Answer to that.
        Say either, and I'll stay the circumstance.
        Let me be satisfied, is't good or bad?

        NURSE: Well, you have made a simple choice; you know not how to
        choose a man. Romeo? No, not he. Though his face be better than
40   any man's, yet his leg excels all men's; and for a hand and a foot,
        and a body, though they be not to be talk'd on, yet they are past
        compare. He is not the flower of courtesy, but, I'll warrant him,
        as gentle as a lamb. Go thy ways, wench; serve God. What, have
        you din'd at home?

45   JUL: No, no. But all this did I know before.
        What says he of our marriage? What of that?

        NURSE: Lord, how my head aches! What a head have I!
        It beats as it would fall in twenty pieces.
        My back o' t' other side,—ah, my back, my back!
50   Beshrew your heart for sending me about
        To catch my death with jaunting up and down!

        JUL: I' faith, I am sorry that thou art not well.
        Sweet, sweet, sweet Nurse, tell me, what says my love?

        NURSE: Your love says, like an honest gentleman, and a courteous, and
55   a kind, and a handsome; and, I warrant, a virtuous—Where is
        your mother?

106

NURSE: *I am weary; give me space for a while. Shame, how my bones ache! What a trip I have had!*

JUL: *I wish you had my bones, and I your news. No, come, I ask you to speak. Good, Nurse, speak.*

NURSE: *Lord, what haste! Can you not wait a while? Do you not see that I am out of breath?*

JUL: *How can you be out of breath when you have breath enough to say to me that you are out of breath? The excuse that you make in this delay is longer than the tale you excuse yourself from telling. Is your news good or bad? Answer to that. Say either, and I'll handle the circumstances. Let me be satisfied; is it good or bad?*

NURSE: *Well, you have made a foolish choice; you don't know how to choose a man. Romeo? No, not he. Though his face be better than any man's, and his physique exceeds all men's; and for a hand and a foot, and a body—though they don't need to be mentioned—since they are beyond compare. He is not the flower of courtesy but, I'll promise him, as gentle as a lamb. Go your ways, girl; enough of this. What, have you dined at home?*

JUL: *No, no. But all this I knew before. What does he say of our marriage? What of that?*

NURSE. *Lord, how my head aches! What a head I have! It beats as it would fall into twenty pieces. My back on the other side—ah, my back, my back! Shame on your heart for sending me about to catch my death with running up and down!*

JUL: *Really, I am sorry that you are not well. Sweet, sweet, sweet Nurse, tell me, what says my love?*

NURSE: *Your love says, like an honest gentleman, and a courteous, and a kind one, and a handsome one; and, I warrant, a virtuous—where is your mother?*

Jul: Where is my mother? Why, she is within.
    Where should she be? How oddly thou reply'st!
    'Your love says, like an honest gentleman,
60   "Where is your mother?"'

Nurse: O God's Lady dear!
    Are you so hot? Marry come up, I trow.
    Is this the poultice for my aching bones?
    Henceforward do your messages yourself.

65   Jul: Here's such a coil! Come, what says Romeo?

Nurse: Have you got leave to go to shrift to-day?

Jul: I have.

Nurse: Then hie you hence to Friar Laurence' cell;
    There stays a husband to make you a wife.
70   Now comes the wanton blood up in your cheeks:
    They'll be in scarlet straight at any news.
    Hie you to church; I must another way,
    To fetch a ladder, by the which your love
    Must climb a bird's nest soon when it is dark.
75   I am the drudge, and toil in your delight;
    But you shall bear the burden soon at night.
    Go; I'll to dinner; hie you to the cell.

Jul: Hie to high fortune! Honest Nurse, farewell.   *[Exeunt.]*

JUL: Where is my mother? Why, she is within. Where should she be? How oddly you reply! "Your love says, like an honest gentleman, 'Where is your mother?'"

NURSE: Oh, God's Lady, dear! Are you so hasty? Please wait up. Is this the remedy for my aching bones? From now on, get your own messages.

JUL: Here's such a fuss! Come, what does Romeo say?

NURSE: Have you gotten permission to go to confession today?

JUL: I have.

NURSE: Then go to Friar Laurence's cell; a husband waits there to make you a wife. Now comes a wanton blush up in your cheeks. They'll be scarlet right away at any news. Go to the church; I must go another way, to fetch a ladder by which your love must climb to get a bird's nest when it is dark. I am the drudge and toil in your pleasure, but you shall bear the burden soon at night. Go; I'll go to dinner. Get you to the cell.

JUL: Go to high fortune! Honest Nurse, good-bye. [Exit.]

SCENE VI
Friar Laurence's cell.

[Enter Friar Laurence and Romeo.]

FRIAR: So smile the heavens upon this holy act
    That after-hours with sorrow chide us not!

ROM: Amen, amen! But come what sorrow can,
    It cannot countervail the exchange of joy
5   That one short minute gives me in her sight.
    Do thou but close our hands with holy words,
    Then love-devouring death do what he dare—
    It is enough I may but call her mine.

FRIAR: These violent delights have violent ends
10   And in their triumph die, like fire and powder,
    Which, as they kiss, consume. The sweetest honey
    Is loathsome in his own deliciousness
    And in the taste confounds the appetite.
    Therefore love moderately: long love doth so;
15   Too swift arrives as tardy as too slow.

[Enter Juliet.]
    Here comes the Lady. O, so light a foot
    Will ne'er wear out the everlasting flint.
    A lover may bestride the gossamer
    That idles in the wanton summer air,
20   And yet not fall; so light is vanity.

JUL: Good even to my ghostly confessor.

FRIAR: Romeo shall thank thee, daughter, for us both.

JUL: As much to him, else is his thanks too much.

SCENE VI
Friar Laurence's cell.

[Enter Friar Laurence and Romeo.]

FRIAR: May the heavens smile upon this holy act so that in future hours we do not repent with sorrow!

ROM: Amen, amen! But come what sorrow may, it cannot equal the exchange of joy that one short minute gives me in her sight. Join our hands with holy words; then love-devouring death may do whatever it dares. It is enough that I may but call her mine.

FRIAR: These violent delights may have violent ends. Fire and powder meet, explode, and die in their triumph. The sweetest honey is loathsome in its own deliciousness and in the taste, confuses the appetite. Therefore, love moderately. Long-lived love does so; too swift a love is as much a problem as too slow.

[Enter Juliet.]
Here comes the lady. Her foot is so light that it will never wear out life's road. A lover may ride the gossamer threads that hang idle in the summer air, and yet not fall—just so light and flimsy are earthly pleasures.

JUL: Good evening to my ghostly confessor.

FRIAR: Romeo shall thank you, daughter, for us both.

JUL: Good evening to him also; otherwise, his thanks would be too much payment.

Rom: Ah, Juliet, if the measure of thy joy
25 Be heap'd like mine, and that thy skill be more
 To blazon it, then sweeten with thy breath
 This neighbour air, and let rich music's tongue
 Unfold the imagin'd happiness that both
 Receive in either by this dear encounter.

30 Jul: Conceit, more rich in matter than in words,
 Brags of his substance, not of ornament.
 They are but beggars that can count their worth;
 But my true love is grown to such excess,
 I cannot sum up sum of half my wealth.

35 Friar: Come, come with me, and we will make short work;
 For, by your leaves, you shall not stay alone
 Till Holy Church incorporate two in one. *[Exeunt.]*

ROM: *Yes, Juliet, if your joy be as great as mine, and your skill be more to speak it, then sweeten with your breath this neighborly air and let your tongue unfold the imagined happiness that we both receive at this meeting.*

JUL: *Conceit, more rich in matter than in words, brags of his substance, not of ornament. But they are beggars that can count their worth; my true love is grown to such excess that I cannot add up even half of my new wealth.*

FRIAR: *Come, come with me, and we will make short work of this, for you shall not stay alone until Holy Church incorporate two in one.* [Exit.]

ACT III

SCENE I

A public place.

[*Enter Mercutio, Benvolio, and Men.*]

BEN: I pray thee, good Mercutio, let's retire.
　　The day is hot, the Capulets abroad.
　　And if we meet, we shall not scape a brawl,
　　For now, these hot days, is the mad blood stirring.

5　　MER: Thou art like one of these fellows that, when he enters the
　　confines of a tavern, claps me his sword upon the table and says
　　'God send me no need of thee!' and by the operation of the second
　　cup draws him on the drawer, when indeed there is no need.

BEN: Am I like such a fellow?

10　　MER: Come, come, thou art as hot a jack in thy mood as any in Italy;
　　and as soon moved to be moody, and as soon moody to be moved.

BEN: And what to?

MER: Nay, an there were two such, we should have none shortly, for
　　one would kill the other. Thou! why, thou wilt quarrel with a man
15　　that hath a hair more or a hair less in his beard than thou hast.
　　Thou wilt quarrel with a man for cracking nuts, having no other
　　reason but because thou hast hazel eyes. What eye but such an eye
　　would spy out such a quarrel? Thy head is as full of quarrels as an
　　egg is full of meat; and yet thy head hath been beaten as addle as
20　　an egg for quarrelling. Thou hast quarrell'd with a man for

ACT III

SCENE I
A public place.

[Enter Mercutio, Benvolio, and Men.]

BEN: *I say to you, good Mercutio, let's leave. The day is hot; the Capulets are all about, and if we should meet them, we shall not escape a brawl, for now, in these hot days, everyone's mad blood is stirring.*

MER: *You are like one of those fellows that, when he enters the confines of a tavern, dumps his sword upon the table and says, "God send me no need of you!" And by the drinking of the second cup, he draws on the waiter, when indeed there was no need.*

BEN: *Am I really like such a fellow?*

MER: *Come, come, you are as hot a man in your mood as any in Italy: easily moved to be moody, and moody to be moved.*

BEN: *And to what purpose?*

MER: *Well, were there two such as you, we should have none shortly, for one would kill the other. You! Why, you will quarrel with a man that has a hair more or a hair less in his beard than you have. You will quarrel with a man for cracking nuts, having no other reason but because you have hazel eyes. What eye but such as your eye would spy out such a quarrel? Your head is as full of quarrels as an egg is full of food; and yet your head has been beaten and is as mixed as an egg for quarreling. You have quarreled with a man for coughing in the street because he woke your dog that was asleep in the sun.*

coughing in the street, because he hath wakened thy dog that hath
lain asleep in the sun. Didst thou not fall out with a tailor for
wearing his new doublet before Easter, with another for tying his
new shoes with an old riband? And yet thou wilt tutor me from
25   quarrelling!

BEN: An I were so apt to quarrel as thou art, any man should buy the
fee simple of my life for an hour and a quarter.

MER: The fee simple? O simple!

[Enter Tybalt and others.]

BEN: By my head, here come the Capulets.

30   MER: By my heel, I care not.

TYB: Follow me close, for I will speak to them.
Gentlemen, good den. A word with one of you.

MER: And but one word with one of us?
Couple it with something; make it a word and a blow.

35   TYB: You shall find me apt enough to that, sir, an you will give me
occasion.

MER: Could you not take some occasion without giving?

TYB: Mercutio, thou consortest with Romeo.

MER: Consort? What, dost thou make us minstrels? An thou make
40   minstrels of us, look to hear nothing but discords. Here's my
fiddlestick; here's that shall make you dance. Zounds, consort!

BEN: We talk here in the public haunt of men.
Either withdraw unto some private place
And reason coldly of your grievances,
45   Or else depart. Here all eyes gaze on us.

Did you not fall out with a tailor for wearing his new doublet before Easter, with another for tying his new shoes with an old ribbon? And yet you will teach me to avoid quarreling!

BEN: If I were as likely to quarrel as you are, any man should take my life within an hour and a quarter, or a simple fee.

MER: The fee simple? Very simple!

[Enter Tybalt and others.]

BEN: By my head, here come the Capulets.

MER: By my heel, I don't care.

TYB: Follow me closely, for I will speak to them. Gentlemen, good day. A word with one of you.

MER: Only one word with one of us? Couple it with something; make it a word and a blow.

TYB: You shall find me ready enough for that, sir, if you will give me reason.

MER: Could you not find some excuse without me giving one?

TYB: Mercutio, you hang out with Romeo.

MER: Hang out? What, do you make us minstrels? If you make minstrels of us, look to hear nothing but discord. Here's my fiddlestick; here's what shall make you dance. By God, hang out!

BEN: We are talking here in a public street. Either withdraw unto some private place and speak of your grievances without hatred, or else depart. Here all eyes gaze on us.

MER: Men's eyes were made to look, and let them gaze.
    I will not budge for no man's pleasure, I.

[Enter Romeo]

TYB: Well, peace be with you, sir. Here comes my man.

MER: But I'll be hang'd, sir, if he wear your livery.
50   Marry, go before to field, he'll be your follower!
    Your worship in that sense may call him man.

TYB: Romeo, the love I bear thee can afford
    No better term than this: thou art a villain.

ROM: Tybalt, the reason that I have to love thee
55   Doth much excuse the appertaining rage
    To such a greeting. Villain am I none.
    Therefore farewell. I see thou knowest me not.

TYB: Boy, this shall not excuse the injuries
    That thou hast done me; therefore turn and draw.

60 ROM: I do protest I never injur'd thee,
    But love thee better than thou canst devise
    Till thou shalt know the reason of my love;
    And so good Capulet, which name I tender
    As dearly as mine own, be satisfied.

65 MER: O calm, dishonourable, vile submission!
    Alla stoccata carries it away. [Draws.]
    Tybalt, you ratcatcher, will you walk?

TYB: What would'st thou have with me?

MER: Good King of Cats, nothing but one of your nine lives. That I
70 mean to make bold withal, and, as you shall use me hereafter, dry-
beat the rest of the eight. Will you pluck your sword out of his
pitcher by the ears? Make haste, lest mine be about your ears ere it be
out.

MER: Men's eyes were made to look, and let them gaze. I will not budge for any man's pleasure, not I.

[Enter Romeo]

TYB: Well, peace be with you, sir. Here comes my man.

MER: I'll be hanged, sir, if he wears your colors. But, go on to the battlefield; he'll follow! In that sense, he's your man.

TYB: Romeo, the love I bear you can afford no better term than this: you are a villain.

ROM: Tybalt, the reason that I have to love you serves to excuse any rage I feel at such a greeting. I am no villain. Therefore, farewell. I see you do not know me.

TYB: Boy, this shall not excuse the injuries that you have done to me; therefore, turn and draw your sword.

ROM: I do protest I never hurt you; in fact, I love you better than you can know, until I can speak the reason of my love. So, good Capulet, whose name I cherish as dearly as my own, be satisfied.

MER: Oh, calm, dishonorable, foul coward! My swordthrust will carry your cowardice away. [Draws.]
Tybalt, you ratcatcher, will you walk with me?

TYB: What do you want with me?

MER: Good King of Cats, nothing but one of your nine lives. I mean to make bold with you; and, if you shall fight me hereafter, beat the rest. Will you pluck your sword out of its case by the hilt? Make haste, or mine will come around your ears before yours is out.

Tyb: I am for you.   *[Draws.]*

75   Rom: Gentle Mercutio, put thy rapier up.

Mer: Come, sir, your passado!   *[They fight.]*

Rom: Draw, Benvolio; beat down their weapons.
    Gentlemen, for shame! forbear this outrage!
    Tybalt, Mercutio, the Prince expressly hath
80   Forbid this bandying in Verona streets.
    Hold, Tybalt! Good Mercutio!

[Tybalt under Romeo's arm thrusts Mercutio in, and flies with his Followers.]

Mer: I am hurt.
    A plague o' both your houses! I am sped.
    Is he gone and hath nothing?

85   Ben: What, art thou hurt?

Mer: Ay, ay, a scratch, a scratch. Marry, 'tis enough.
    Where is my page? Go, villain, fetch a surgeon.   *[Exit Page.]*

Rom: Courage, man. The hurt cannot be much.

Mer: No, 'tis not so deep as a well, nor so wide as a church door; but
90   'tis enough, 'twill serve. Ask for me to-morrow, and you shall find
    me a grave man. I am peppered, I warrant, for this world. A plague
    o' both your houses! Zounds, a dog, a rat, a mouse, a cat, to
    scratch a man to death! a braggart, a rogue, a villain, that fights by
    the book of arithmetic! Why the devil came you between us? I was
95   hurt under your arm.

Rom: I thought all for the best.

Mer: Help me into some house, Benvolio,
    Or I shall faint. A plague o' both your houses!
    They have made worms' meat of me. I have it,
100   And soundly too. Your houses!   *[Exit, supported by Benvolio.]*

120

TYB: *I am ready for you.*   [Draws.]

ROM: *Gentle Mercutio, put your rapier up.*

MER: *Come, sir, your swordplay.*   [They fight.]

ROM: *Draw, Benvolio; beat down their weapons. Gentlemen, for shame! Stop this outrage! Tybalt, Mercutio, the Prince has expressly forbidden this fighting in Verona's streets. Hold, Tybalt! Good Mercutio!*

[Tybalt strikes under Romeo's arm and stabs Mercutio, then leaves with his followers.]

MER: *I am hurt. A plague on both your houses! I am dying. Has Tybalt left without any wounds?*

BEN: *What, are you hurt?*

MER: *Yes, a scratch, a scratch. But it is enough. Where is my page? Go, boy, fetch a surgeon.*   [Exit Page.]

ROM: *Courage, man. The hurt cannot be very much.*

MER: *No, it is not as deep as a well nor as wide as a church door, but it is enough. It will do. Ask for me tomorrow, and you shall find me a grave man. I am finished, I think, with this world. A plague on both your houses! God, a dog, a rat, a mouse, a cat to scratch a man to death! A braggart, a rogue, a villain who fights with such a plan! Why the devil did you come you between us? I was wounded under your arm.*

ROM: *I thought it all for the best to stop the fight.*

MER: *Help me into some house, Benvolio, or I shall faint. A plague on both your houses! They have made worms' meat of me. I have it, and soundly too. A plague on your houses!*   [Exit, supported by Benvolio.]

ROM: This gentleman, the Prince's near ally,
    My very friend, hath got this mortal hurt
    In my behalf—my reputation stain'd
    With Tybalt's slander—Tybalt, that an hour
105   Hath been my kinsman. O sweet Juliet,
    Thy beauty hath made me effeminate
     And in my temper soft'ned valour's steel

[Enter Benvolio.]

BEN: O Romeo, Romeo, brave Mercutio's dead!
    That gallant spirit hath aspir'd the clouds,
110   Which too untimely here did scorn the earth.

ROM: This day's black fate on more days doth depend;
    This but begins the woe others must end.

[Enter Tybalt.]

BEN: Here comes the furious Tybalt back again.

ROM: Alive in triumph, and Mercutio slain?
115   Away to heaven respective lenity,
    And fire-ey'd fury be my conduct now!
    Now, Tybalt, take the 'villain' back again
    That late thou gavest me; for Mercutio's soul
    Is but a little way above our heads,
120   Staying for thine to keep him company.
    Either thou or I, or both, must go with him.

TYB: Thou, wretched boy, that didst consort him here,
    Shalt with him hence.

ROM: This shall determine that.   *[They fight. Tybalt falls.]*

125 BEN: Romeo, away, be gone!
    The citizens are up, and Tybalt slain.
    Stand not amaz'd. The Prince will doom thee death
    If thou art taken. Hence, be gone, away!

ROM: *This gentleman, the Prince's cousin, my friend, has gotten this mortal hurt on my behalf. My reputation is stained with Tybalt's slander—Tybalt, who only for an hour has been my relative. Oh, sweet Juliet, your beauty has made me effeminate, and my nature has softened valor's steel!*

[Enter Benvolio.]

BEN: *Oh, Romeo, Romeo, brave Mercutio's dead! His gallant spirit has ascended to the heavens and left the earth too soon.*

ROM: *From this day's black fate other black days follow; this merely begins the sorrows which others must end.*

[Enter Tybalt.]

BEN: *Here comes the furious Tybalt back again.*

ROM: *Alive in triumph, and Mercutio slain? Gone away to heaven; they take different paths—and fire-eyed fury will be my action now! Now, Tybalt, take the "villain" back again that you called me recently. Mercutio's soul is but a little way above our heads, waiting for yours to keep him company. Either you or I, or both, must go with him.*

TYB: *You, wretched boy, who waited with him here, shall now go with him.*

ROM: *This fight shall determine that.*   [They fight. Tybalt falls.]

BEN: *Romeo, away, be gone! The citizens are up in arms, and Tybalt is slain. Do not stand here amazed. The Prince will doom you to death if you are caught. Leave. Be gone, away!*

ROM: O, I am fortune's fool!

130   BEN: Why dost thou stay?   *[Exit Romeo.]*

[Enter Citizens.]

CITIZEN: Which way ran he that kill'd Mercutio?
        Tybalt, that murderer, which way ran he?

BEN: There lies that Tybalt.

CITIZEN: Up, sir, go with me.
135   I charge thee in the Prince's name obey.

*[Enter Prince (attended), Old Montague, Capulet, their Wives, and
others.]*

PRINCE: Where are the vile beginners of this fray?

BEN: O noble Prince, I can discover all
        The unlucky manage of this fatal brawl.
        There lies the man, slain by young Romeo,
140   That slew thy kinsman, brave Mercutio.

LADY CAP: Tybalt, my cousin! O my brother's child!
        O Prince! O husband! O, the blood is spill'd
        Of my dear kinsman! Prince, as thou art true,
        For blood of ours, shed blood of Montague.
145   O cousin, cousin!

PRINCE: Benvolio, who began this bloody fray?

BEN: Tybalt, here slain, whom Romeo's hand did slay.
        Romeo, that spoke him fair, bid him bethink
        How nice the quarrel was, and urg'd withal
150   Your high displeasure. All this, uttered
        With gentle breath, calm look, knees humbly bow'd,
        Could not take truce with the unruly spleen
        Of Tybalt deaf to peace, but that he tilts
        With piercing steel at bold Mercutio's breast;

ROM: *Oh, I am fortune's fool!*

BEN: *Why do you stay?*   [Exit Romeo.]

[Enter Citizens.]

CITIZEN: *Which way did the man run who killed Mercutio? Tybalt, that murderer, which way did he run?*

BEN: *There lies Tybalt.*

CITIZEN: *Get up, sir, go with me. I charge you in the Prince's name; obey.*

[Enter Prince, with attendants, Old Montague, Capulet, their Wives, and others.]

PRINCE: *Where are the vile people who began this fight?*

BEN: *Oh, noble Prince, I can retell all the events which occurred in this fatal brawl. There lies the man, Tybalt, slain by young Romeo; Tybalt slew your kinsman, brave Mercutio.*

LADY CAP: *Tybalt, my cousin! Oh, my brother's child! Oh, Prince! Oh, husband! Oh, the blood is spilled of my dear kinsman! Prince, as you are honest, blood of ours is shed, and you must now shed blood of Montague. Oh, cousin, cousin!*

PRINCE: *Benvolio, who began this bloody fray?*

BEN: *Tybalt, who lies here dead, had challenged Romeo. Romeo spoke to him fairly, and bid him to think how shallow the quarrel was, and urged also that you would be highly displeased. All this he uttered with gentle breath, calm look, knees humbly bowed—but none of this could pacify Tybalt, who was deaf to it. He struck with piercing steel at bold Mercutio's breast who, equally hot, turned blade against blade and, with a martial scorn, with one hand, beat Tybalt's sword aside and with the other sent it back towards Tybalt, whose dexterity repelled it. Romeo, running between, cried aloud, "Stop,*

125

155   Who, all as hot, turns deadly point to point,
And, with a martial scorn, with one hand beats
Cold death aside and with the other sends
It back to Tybalt, whose dexterity
Retorts it. Romeo he cries aloud,
160   'Hold, friends! friends, part!' and swifter than his tongue,
His agile arm beats down their fatal points,
And 'twixt them rushes; underneath whose arm
An envious thrust from Tybalt hit the life
Of stout Mercutio, and then Tybalt fled;
165   But by-and-by comes back to Romeo,
Who had but newly entertain'd revenge,
And to't they go like lightning; for, ere I
Could draw to part them, was stout Tybalt slain;
And, as he fell, did Romeo turn and fly.
170   This is the truth, or let Benvolio die.

LADY CAP: He is a kinsman to the Montague;
Affection makes him false, he speaks not true.
Some twenty of them fought in this black strife,
And all those twenty could but kill one life.
175   I beg for justice, which thou, Prince, must give.
Romeo slew Tybalt; Romeo must not live.

PRINCE: Romeo slew him; he slew Mercutio.
Who now the price of his dear blood doth owe?

MON: Not Romeo, Prince; he was Mercutio's friend;
180   His fault concludes but what the law should end,
The life of Tybalt.

PRINCE: And for that offence
Immediately we do exile him hence.
I have an interest in your hate's proceeding,
185   My blood for your rude brawls doth lie ableeding;
But I'll amerce you with so strong a fine
That you shall all repent the loss of mine.
I will be deaf to pleading and excuses;
Nor tears nor prayers shall purchase out abuses.
190   Therefore use none. Let Romeo hence in haste,

friends! Friends, part!" And swifter than his tongue, his agile arm beat down
their fatal blades. But then, underneath Romeo's arm, an envious thrust from
Tybalt took the life of stout Mercutio, and then Tybalt fled. Later, he came
back to Romeo, who only then, had thought of revenge, and they went at it
like lightning. Before I could draw to stop them, stout Tybalt was slain; and,
as he fell, Romeo turned and fled. This is the truth, or let Benvolio die.

LADY CAP: He is a kinsman to the Montague; affection makes him lie. He doesn't
speak the truth. Some twenty of them fought in this black strife, and all those
twenty could kill only one life. I beg for justice which you, Prince, must give.
Romeo slew Tybalt; Romeo must not live.

PRINCE: Romeo slew Tybalt; Tybalt slew Mercutio. Who now owes the price that
must be paid with blood?

MON: Not Romeo, Prince; he was Mercutio's friend. He did only what the law
allows when he took the life of Tybalt.

PRINCE: And for that offense we do immediately exile him. I have an interest in
your hateful feud. Because of your rude brawls, my relative lies dead, but
I'll punish you with so strong a fine that you shall all repent my loss. I will
be deaf to pleading and excuses; no tears nor prayers shall buy a pardon for
these crimes. Therefore, use none. Let Romeo leave in haste. Otherwise, when
he is found, that hour will be his last. Bear this body away. Do as we order;
pardoning those who kill will only cause more murders.

[Exit.]

Else, when he is found, that hour is his last.
Bear hence this body, and attend our will.
Mercy but murders, pardoning those that kill.   *[Exeunt.]*

SCENE II
Capulet's orchard.

[Enter Juliet alone.]

JUL: Gallop apace, you fiery-footed steeds,
 Towards Phoebus' lodging! Such a wagoner
 As Phaeton would whip you to the west
 And bring in cloudy night immediately.
5 Spread thy close curtain, love-performing night,
 That runaway eyes may wink, and Romeo
 Leap to these arms untalk'd of and unseen.
 Lovers can see to do their amorous rites
 By their own beauties; or, if love be blind,
10 It best agrees with night. Come, civil night,
 Thou sober-suited matron, all in black,
 And learn me how to lose a winning match,
 Play'd for a pair of stainless maidenhoods.
 Hood my unmann'd blood, bating in my cheeks,
15 With thy black mantle till strange love, grown bold,
 Think true love acted simple modesty.
 Come, night; come, Romeo; come, thou day in night;
 For thou wilt lie upon the wings of night
 Whiter than new snow upon a raven's back.
20 Come, gentle night; come, loving, black-brow'd night;
 Give me my Romeo; and, when he shall die,
 Take him and cut him out in little stars,
 And he will make the face of heaven so fine
 That all the world will be in love with night
25 And pay no worship to the garish sun.
 O, I have bought the mansion of a love,
 But not possess'd it; and though I am sold,
 Not yet enjoy'd. So tedious is this day

SCENE II

Capulet's orchard.

[Enter Juliet alone.]

JUL: *Gallop quickly, you fiery-footed horses, towards the night! Such a speedy driver as Phaeton would whip you to the West and bring in cloudy night immediately. Spread your concealing curtain, love-performing night, so runaway eyes may be closed, and Romeo will leap into these arms without being talked of or seen by anyone. Lovers can see to do their loving by the light of their own beauties, and, if love is blind, it agrees with night. Come, civil night, you sober-suited lady, all in black, and teach me how to lose this winning match, played by a pair of stainless virgins. Cover my wild blood, waiting in my cheeks, with your black mantle of night. Strange love grows bold, and true love acts with simple modesty. Come, night; come, Romeo; come, turn day into night. You will seem, upon the wings of night, whiter than new snow upon a raven's back. Come, gentle night. Come, loving, black-browed night; give me my Romeo. When he shall die, take him and cut him out in little stars, and he will make the face of heaven so fine that all the world will be in love with night and pay no worship to the garish sun. Oh, I have bought the mansion of a love, but have not yet possessed it. Though I have been sold, I have not yet been enjoyed by Romeo. This day has become as tedious as the night before some festival is to an impatient child who has new clothes and may not wear them. Oh, here comes my Nurse, and she brings news. Every tongue that speaks Romeo's name speaks with heavenly eloquence.* [Enter Nurse, with cords.] *Now, Nurse, what news? What have you there? The cords that Romeo asked you fetch?*

As is the night before some festival
30   To an impatient child that hath new robes
And may not wear them. O, here comes my Nurse,
And she brings news; and every tongue that speaks
But Romeo's name speaks heavenly eloquence.
[Enter Nurse, with cords.]
Now, Nurse, what news? What hast thou there? the cords
35   That Romeo bid thee fetch?

NURSE: Ay, ay, the cords.   *[Throws them down.]*

JUL: Ay me! what news? Why dost thou wring thy hands?

NURSE: Ah, well-a-day! he's dead, he's dead, he's dead!
We are undone, lady, we are undone!
40   Alack the day! he's gone, he's kill'd, he's dead!

JUL: Can heaven be so envious?

NURSE: Romeo can,
Though heaven cannot. O Romeo, Romeo!
Who ever would have thought it? Romeo!

45   JUL: What devil art thou that dost torment me thus?
This torture should be roar'd in dismal hell.
Hath Romeo slain himself? Say thou but 'I,'
And that bare vowel 'I' shall poison more
Than the death-darting eye of cockatrice.
50   I am not I, if there be such an 'I';
Or those eyes shut that make thee answer 'I.'
If he be slain, say 'I'; or if not, 'no.'
Brief sounds determine of my weal or woe.

NURSE: I saw the wound, I saw it with mine eyes,
55   (God save the mark!) here on his manly breast.
A piteous corse, a bloody piteous corse;
Pale, pale as ashes, all bedaub'd in blood,
All in gore-blood. I swounded at the sight.

NURSE: Ay, ay, the cords.   [Throws them down.]

JUL: Ay me! What news? Why do you wring your hands?

NURSE: Oh, alas! He's dead, he's dead, he's dead! We are undone, lady, we are ruined! Woe is the day! He's gone, he's killed, he's dead!

JUL: Can heaven be so wicked?

NURSE: Romeo can, though heaven cannot. Oh, Romeo, Romeo! Who ever would have thought it? Romeo!

JUL: What devil are you that torments me thus? This torture should be roared in dismal hell. Has Romeo slain himself? Say only "I," and that bare vowel "I" shall poison me more than the death eye of a serpent. I am not I, if there is such an "I," or Romeo's death makes you answer "I." If he is slain, say "I," or if not, "no." Brief sounds determine my wellness or grief.

NURSE: I saw the wound, I saw it with my eyes, (God save the mark!) here on his manly breast. A piteous corpse, a bloody, piteous corpse; pale, pale as ashes, all speckled with blood, all in gore-blood. I was faint at the sight.

JUL: O, break, my heart! poor bankrout, break at once!
60   To prison, eyes; ne'er look on liberty!
     Vile earth, to earth resign; end motion here,
     And thou and Romeo press one heavy bier!

NURSE: O Tybalt, Tybalt, the best friend I had!
     O courteous Tybalt! honest gentleman
65   That ever I should live to see thee dead!

JUL: What storm is this that blows so contrary?
     Is Romeo slaught'red, and is Tybalt dead?
     My dear-lov'd cousin, and my dearer lord?
     Then, dreadful trumpet, sound the general doom!
70   For who is living, if those two are gone?

NURSE: Tybalt is gone, and Romeo banished;
     Romeo that kill'd him, he is banished.

JUL: O God! Did Romeo's hand shed Tybalt's blood?

NURSE: It did, it did! alas the day, it did!

75   JUL: O serpent heart, hid with a flow'ring face!
     Did ever dragon keep so fair a cave?
     Beautiful tyrant! fiend angelical!
     Dove-feather'd raven! wolvish-ravening lamb!
     Despised substance of divinest show!
80   Just opposite to what thou justly seem'st—
     A damned saint, an honourable villain!
     O nature, what hadst thou to do in hell
     When thou didst bower the spirit of a fiend
     In mortal paradise of such sweet flesh?
85   Was ever book containing such vile matter
     So fairly bound? O, that deceit should dwell
     In such a gorgeous palace!

NURSE: There's no trust,
     No faith, no honesty in men; all perjur'd,
90   All forsworn, all naught, all dissemblers.
     Ah, where's my man? Give me some aqua vitae.

JUL: Oh, break, my heart! Poor bankruptcy, break at once! To prison, eyes; never again look on liberty! Vile body, be consigned to the earth; end motion here, and you and Romeo press one heavy casket!

NURSE: Oh, Tybalt, Tybalt, the best friend I had! Oh, courteous Tybalt! Honest gentleman, that ever I should live to see you dead!

JUL: What storm is this that blows so strangely? Is Romeo slaughtered, and is Tybalt dead? My dear-loved cousin, and my dearer lord? Then, dreadful trumpet, sound the general doom! For who can live if those two are gone?

NURSE: Tybalt is gone, and Romeo banished; Romeo who killed him, he is banished.

JUL: Oh, God! Did Romeo's hand shed Tybalt's blood?

NURSE: It did, it did! Alas the day, it did!

JUL: Oh, what a serpent heart is hidden within a flowering face! Did ever a dragon keep so fair a cave as Romeo? Romeo the beautiful tyrant! Angelic fiend! Dove-feathered raven! Wolf-eating lamb! Despised substance of most heavenly appearance, just opposite to what you seemed to be—a damned saint, an honorable villain! Oh, nature, what had you to do in hell when you placed the spirit of a fiend in such heavenly sweet flesh? Was ever a book containing such vile matter so beautifully bound? Oh, that deceit should dwell in such a gorgeous palace!

NURSE: There's no trust, no faith, no honesty in men; all have perjured, all swear falsely, all are wicked, all are liars. Ah, where's my man? Give me some spirits. These griefs, these woes, these sorrows make me feel old. May shame come to Romeo!

These griefs, these woes, these sorrows make me old.
Shame come to Romeo!

Jul: Blister'd be thy tongue
95   For such a wish! He was not born to shame.
Upon his brow shame is asham'd to sit;
For 'tis a throne where honour may be crown'd
Sole monarch of the universal earth.
O, what a beast was I to chide at him!

100   Nurse: Will you speak well of him that kill'd your cousin?

Jul: Shall I speak ill of him that is my husband?
Ah, poor my lord, what tongue shall smooth thy name
When I, thy three-hours' wife, have mangled it?
But wherefore, villain, didst thou kill my cousin?
105   That villain cousin would have kill'd my husband.
Back, foolish tears, back to your native spring!
Your tributary drops belong to woe,
Which you, mistaking, offer up to joy.
My husband lives, that Tybalt would have slain;
110   And Tybalt's dead, that would have slain my husband.
All this is comfort; wherefore weep I then?
Some word there was, worser than Tybalt's death,
That murdered me. I would forget it fain;
But O, it presses to my memory
115   Like damned guilty deeds to sinners' minds!
'Tybalt is dead, and Romeo banished.'
That 'banished,' that one word 'banished,'
Hath slain ten thousand Tybalts. Tybalt's death
Was woe enough, if it had ended there;
120   Or, if sour woe delights in fellowship
And needly will be rank'd with other griefs,
Why followed not, when she said 'Tybalt's dead,'
Thy father, or thy mother, nay, or both,
Which modern lamentation might have mov'd?
125   But with a rearward following Tybalt's death,
'Romeo is banished'—to speak that word
Is father, mother, Tybalt, Romeo, Juliet,
All slain, all dead. 'Romeo is banished'—

JUL.: *May your tongue be blistered for such a wish! He was not born to shame. Upon his brow shame is ashamed to sit, for it is a throne where honor may be crowned the sole ruler of the universal earth. Oh, what a beast was I to speak harshly of him!*

NURSE: *Will you speak well of him who has killed your cousin?*

JUL.: *Shall I speak ill of him that is my husband? Ah, my poor lord. Whose tongue shall smooth your name when I, your wife of three hours, have mangled it? But why, villain, did you kill my cousin? But that villain cousin would have killed my husband. Back, foolish tears, back to your original spring! Your watery drops belong to my woe, which you, mistakenly, offer up as joy. My husband lives, whom Tybalt would have slain; and Tybalt's dead, who would have slain my husband. All this is comforting. Why then do I weep? Some word there was, worse than Tybalt's death, that murdered me. I would like to forget it, but Oh, it presses down on my memory like guilty deeds do on sinners' minds!*

"Tybalt is dead, and Romeo banished." That "banished," that one word "banished," has slain ten thousand Tybalts. Tybalt's death was woe enough if it had ended there. If sour woe delights in fellowship, and grief needs to be grouped with other griefs, why when she said, "Tybalt's dead," she did not follow it with news that my father, or my mother, or both, are dead? That would have provoked a normal flow of tears. But why must the addition following Tybalt's death be, "Romeo is banished!"? To say that Romeo is banished is as bad as saying that father, mother, Tybalt, Romeo, and Juliet, all are slain, all dead. "Romeo is banished"—there is no end, no limit, measure, boundary in that word's death; no words can give voice to that woe. Where is my father and my mother, Nurse?

There is no end, no limit, measure, bound,
130   In that word's death; no words can that woe sound.
Where is my father and my mother, Nurse?

NURSE: Weeping and wailing over Tybalt's corse.
Will you go to them? I will bring you thither.

JUL: Wash they his wounds with tears? Mine shall be spent,
135   When theirs are dry, for Romeo's banishment.
Take up those cords. Poor ropes, you are beguil'd,
Both you and I, for Romeo is exil'd.
He made you for a highway to my bed;
But I, a maid, die maiden-widowed.
140   Come, cords; come, Nurse. I'll to my wedding bed;
And death, not Romeo, take my maidenhead!

NURSE: Hie to your chamber. I'll find Romeo
To comfort you. I wot well where he is.
Hark ye, your Romeo will be here at night.
145   I'll to him; he is hid at Laurence' cell.

JUL: O, find him! give this ring to my true knight
And bid him come to take his last farewell.   *[Exeunt.]*

NURSE: *Weeping and wailing over Tybalt's corpse. Will you go to them? I will bring you there.*

JUL: *Do they wash his wounds with their tears? Mine shall be given for Romeo's banishment long after theirs are dry. Take up those cords. Poor ropes, you are tricked, just as I am, for Romeo is exiled. He made you to be a highway to my bed, but I, a maid, will die a widow. Come, cords; come, Nurse. I'll go to my wedding bed; and death, not Romeo, will take my virginity!*

NURSE: *Get to your chamber. I'll find Romeo to comfort you. I know where he is. Listen, your Romeo will be here this evening. I'll go to him; he is hidden at Friar Laurence's cell.*

JUL: *Oh, find him! Give this ring to my true knight and bid him come to take his last good-bye.*   [Exit.]

SCENE III
Friar Laurence's Cell.

[Enter Friar Laurence.]

FRIAR: Romeo, come forth; come forth, thou fearful man.
    Affliction is enamour'd of thy parts,
    And thou art wedded to calamity.

[Enter Romeo.]

ROM: Father, what news? What is the Prince's doom?
5   What sorrow craves acquaintance at my hand
    That I yet know not?

FRIAR: Too familiar
    Is my dear son with such sour company.
    I bring thee tidings of the Prince's doom.

10   ROM: What less than doomsday is the Prince's doom?

FRIAR: A gentler judgment vanish'd from his lips—
    Not body's death, but body's banishment.

ROM: Ha, banishment? Be merciful, say 'death';
    For exile hath more terror in his look,
15   Much more than death. Do not say 'banishment.'

FRIAR: Hence from Verona art thou banished.
    Be patient, for the world is broad and wide.

ROM: There is no world without Verona walls,
    But purgatory, torture, hell itself.
20   Hence banished is banish'd from the world,
    And world's exile is death. Then 'banishment'
    Is death misterm'd. Calling death 'banishment,'
    Thou cut'st my head off with a golden axe
    And smilest upon the stroke that murders me.

SCENE III

Friar Laurence's Cell.

[Enter Friar Laurence.]

FRIAR: *Romeo, come out; come out, you fearful man. Affliction loves you, and you are wed to calamity.*

[Enter Romeo.]

ROM: *Father, what news? What is the Prince's judgment? What sorrow that I do not know now do I need to deal with?*

FRIAR: *You are too familiar, my dear son, with such sour news. I bring you news of the Prince's sentence.*

ROM: *Is the Prince's verdict less than death?*

FRIAR: *A gentler judgment came from his lips—not your body's death, but your body's banishment.*

ROM: *Ah, banishment? Be merciful, say, "death," for exile has more terror for me than death. Do not say "banishment."*

FRIAR: *From Verona you are now banished. Be patient, for the world is broad and wide.*

ROM: *There is no world outside Verona walls but purgatory, torture, hell itself. Being banished from here is to be banished from the world, and the world's exile is death. Then "banishment" is only death misnamed. Calling death "banishment," you cut my head off with a golden axe and smile upon the stroke that murders me.*

139

25   FRIAR: O deadly sin! O rude unthankfulness!
          Thy fault our law calls death; but the kind Prince,
          Taking thy part, hath rush'd aside the law,
          And turn'd that black word death to banishment.
          This is dear mercy, and thou seest it not.

30   ROM: 'Tis torture, and not mercy. Heaven is here,
          Where Juliet lives; and every cat and dog
          And little mouse, every unworthy thing,
          Live here in heaven and may look on her;
          But Romeo may not. More validity,
35   More honourable state, more courtship lives
          In carrion flies than Romeo. They may seize
          On the white wonder of dear Juliet's hand
          And steal immortal blessing from her lips,
          Who, even in pure and vestal modesty,
40   Still blush, as thinking their own kisses sin;
          But Romeo may not—he is banished.
          This may flies do, when I from this must fly;
          They are free men, but I am banished.
          And sayest thou yet that exile is not death?
45   Hadst thou no poison mix'd, no sharp-ground knife,
          No sudden mean of death, though ne'er so mean,
          But 'banished' to kill me—'banished'?
          O friar, the damned use that word in hell;
          Howling attends it! How hast thou the heart,
50   Being a divine, a ghostly confessor,
          A sin-absolver, and my friend profess'd,
          To mangle me with that word 'banished'?

      FRIAR: Thou fond mad man, hear me a little speak.

      ROM: O, thou wilt speak again of banishment.

55   FRIAR: I'll give thee armour to keep off that word;
          Adversity's sweet milk, philosophy,
          To comfort thee, though thou art banished.

FRIAR: *Romeo, you commit a deadly sin of rude unthankfulness! Our law punishes your crime by death, but the kind Prince, taking your side, has brushed aside the law and turned that black word death to banishment. This is dear mercy, and you don't see it.*

ROM: *It is torture, and not mercy. Heaven is here, where Juliet lives, and every cat and dog and little mouse, every unworthy thing, lives here in heaven and may look upon her, but Romeo may not. More validity, more honorable state, more courtship lives in garbage flies than in Romeo. They may seize on the white wonder of dear Juliet's hand and steal immortal blessing from her lips, which, even in pure and vestal modesty, still blush, as if thinking their own kisses are sins, but Romeo may not—he is banished. This may flies do, but I must fly from this; they are free, but I am banished. And yet you say that exile is not death? No poison had you mixed, no sharply ground knife, no sudden means of death can ever be so mean since "banished" is to kill me. "Banished"? Oh, friar, the damned use that word in hell; howling goes with it! How have you the heart, being a divine, a ghostly confessor, a sin-absolver, and my professed friend, to mangle me with that word "banished"?*

FRIAR: *You fond madman, hear me speak a little.*

ROM: *Oh, you will speak again of banishment.*

FRIAR: *I'll give you the armor to ward off that word; I'll give adversity's sweet milk, philosophy, which shall comfort you, even though you are banished.*

141

ROM: Yet 'banished'? Hang up philosophy!
    Unless philosophy can make a Juliet,
60   Displant a town, reverse a prince's doom,
    It helps not, it prevails not. Talk no more.

FRIAR: O, then I see that madmen have no ears.

ROM: How should they, when that wise men have no eyes?

FRIAR: Let me dispute with thee of thy estate.

65 ROM: Thou canst not speak of that thou dost not feel.
    Wert thou as young as I, Juliet thy love,
    An hour but married, Tybalt murdered,
    Doting like me, and like me banished,
    Then mightst thou speak, then mightst thou tear thy hair,
70   And fall upon the ground, as I do now,
    Taking the measure of an unmade grave. *[Knock within.]*

FRIAR: Arise; one knocks. Good Romeo, hide thyself.

ROM: Not I; unless the breath of heartsick groans,
    Mist-like infold me from the search of eyes.   *[Knock.]*

75 FRIAR: Hark, how they knock! Who's there? Romeo, arise;
    Thou wilt be taken.—Stay awhile!—Stand up;   *[Knock.]*
    Run to my study.—By-and-by!—God's will,
    What simpleness is this.—I come, I come!   *[Knock.]*
    Who knocks so hard? Whence come you? What's your will

80 NURSE: *[Within.]* Let me come in, and you shall know my errand. I
    come from Lady Juliet.

FRIAR: Welcome, then.

[Enter Nurse.]

NURSE: O holy friar, O, tell me, holy friar
    Where is my lady's lord, where's Romeo?

ROM: But "banished"? Execute your philosophy! Unless philosophy can make a Juliet, transplant a town, or reverse a prince's judgment, it does not help, it does not sway. Talk no more.

FRIAR: Oh, then I see that madmen have no ears.

ROM: How should they when wise men have no eyes?

FRIAR: Let me argue with you about your situation.

ROM: You cannot speak of that which you do not feel. Were you as young as I, Juliet your love, married only an hour, Tybalt murdered, feeling like me, and like me banished, then you might speak. Then might you tear your hair and fall upon the ground as I do now, measuring an unmade grave.

[Knock within.]

FRIAR: Arise; someone knocks. Good Romeo, hide yourself.

ROM: Not I, unless the breath of heartsick groans, like mist, will hide me from the search of eyes.   [Knock.]

FRIAR: Listen, how they knock! Who's there? Romeo, arise; you will be taken.— Stay awhile!—Stand up; [Knock.] Quick, Romeo, run to my study.—By-and-by!—God's will, what simpleness is this.—I come, I come! [Knock.] Who knocks so hard? Where do you come from? What's your desire?

NURSE: [Within.] Let me come in, and you shall know my errand. I come from Lady Juliet.

FRIAR: Welcome, then.

[Enter Nurse.]

NURSE: Holy friar, tell me, holy friar, where is my lady's lord; where's Romeo?

143

85   FRIAR: There on the ground, with his own tears made drunk.

        NURSE: O, he is even in my mistress' case,
           Just in her case!

        FRIAR: O woeful sympathy!
           Piteous predicament!

90   NURSE: Even so lies she,
           Blubbering and weeping, weeping and blubbering.
           Stand up, stand up! Stand, an you be a man.
           For Juliet's sake, for her sake, rise and stand!
           Why should you fall into so deep an O?

95   ROM: *[Rises.]* Nurse—

        NURSE: Ah sir! ah sir! Well, death's the end of all.

        ROM: Spakest thou of Juliet? How is it with her?
           Doth not she think me an old murderer,
           Now I have stain'd the childhood of our joy
100   With blood remov'd but little from her own?
           Where is she? and how doth she? and what says
           My conceal'd lady to our cancell'd love?

        NURSE: O, she says nothing, sir, but weeps and weeps;
           And now falls on her bed, and then starts up,
105   And Tybalt calls; and then on Romeo cries,
           And then down falls again.

        ROM: As if that name,
           Shot from the deadly level of a gun,
           Did murder her; as that name's cursed hand
110   Murdered her kinsman. O, tell me, friar, tell me,
           In what vile part of this anatomy
           Doth my name lodge? Tell me, that I may sack
           The hateful mansion. *[Draws his dagger.]*

        FRIAR: Hold thy desperate hand.
115   Art thou a man? Thy form cries out thou art;

FRIAR: *There on the ground, made drunk with his own tears.*

NURSE: *Oh, he is in the same state as my mistress, just the same!*

FRIAR: *Oh, woeful sympathy! Piteous predicament!*

NURSE: *Even so she lies, blubbering and weeping, weeping and blubbering. Stand up, stand up! Stand, if you are a man. For Juliet's sake, for her sake, rise and stand! Why should you fall into so deep a groan?*

ROM: [Rises.] *Nurse—*

NURSE: *Ah, sir! Ah, sir! Well, death is the end of all.*

ROM: *Do you speak of Juliet? How is it with her? Does she not think me a murderer now that I have stained the newness of our joy with blood only a little removed from her own? Where is she? And how does she? And what does my concealed lady say to our cancelled love?*

NURSE: *Oh, she says nothing, sir, but weeps and weeps, and immediately she falls on her bed, and then starts up, and calls Tybalt; and then she cries out for Romeo, and then she falls down again.*

ROM: *As if that name, shot from the deadly aim of a gun, did murder her, just as that name's cursed hand murdered her kinsman. Oh, tell me, friar, tell me, in what vile part of this anatomy does my name lodge? Tell me, that I may destroy the hateful spot.* [Draws his dagger.]

FRIAR: *Stop your desperate act. Are you a man? Your form says that you are; your tears are womanish, your wild acts denote the unreasonable fury of a*

Thy tears are womanish, thy wild acts denote
The unreasonable fury of a beast.
Unseemly woman in a seeming man!
Or ill-beseeming beast in seeming both!
120   Thou hast amaz'd me. By my holy order,
I thought thy disposition better temper'd.
Hast thou slain Tybalt? Wilt thou slay thyself?
And slay thy lady that in thy life lives,
By doing damned hate upon thyself?
125   Why railest thou on thy birth, the heaven, and earth?
Since birth and heaven and earth, all three do meet
In thee at once; which thou at once wouldst lose.
Fie, fie, thou shamest thy shape, thy love, thy wit,
Which, like a usurer, abound'st in all,
130   And usest none in that true use indeed
Which should bedeck thy shape, thy love, thy wit.
Thy noble shape is but a form of wax
Digressing from the valour of a man;
Thy dear love sworn but hollow perjury,
135   Killing that love which thou hast vow'd to cherish;
Thy wit, that ornament to shape and love,
Misshapen in the conduct of them both,
Like powder in a skilless soldier's flask,
Is set afire by thine own ignorance,
140   And thou dismemb'red with thine own defence.
What, rouse thee, man! Thy Juliet is alive,
For whose dear sake thou wast but lately dead.
There art thou happy. Tybalt would kill thee,
But thou slewest Tybalt. There art thou happy too.
145   The law, that threat'ned death, becomes thy friend
And turns it to exile. There art thou happy.
A pack of blessings light upon thy back;
Happiness courts thee in her best array;
But, like a misbhav'd and sullen wench,
150   Thou pout'st upon thy fortune and thy love.
Take heed, take heed, for such die miserable.
Go get thee to thy love, as was decreed,
Ascend her chamber, hence and comfort her.
But look thou stay not till the watch be set,
155   For then thou canst not pass to Mantua,

146

beast. You're a woman, though you look like a man! Or else you're a beast and a man and woman! You have amazed me. By my holy order, I thought your disposition more moderate. Have you slain Tybalt? Will you slay yourself? And kill the lady who lives in your life by doing this damned abuse upon yourself? Why do you rant about your birth, the heavens, and the earth? Birth and heaven and earth—all three of them meet in you together at once! You will lose them all. Shame, shame. You shame your body, your love, your wit, like a money lender who has many assets and uses none well. Your noble shape is simply a wax form, straying from the honor of a man; the dear love you profess is a hollow lie, killing the love which you have vowed to cherish; your mind, that instrument to shape and love, is like gunpowder in a skilless soldier's flask; it is fired by your own ignorance, and you are cut up by your own defense. Well, rise, man! Your Juliet is alive, for whose dear sake you were only recently dead. You should be happy. Tybalt would kill you, but you killed Tybalt. You should be happy about that, too. The law, which threatened your death, becomes your friend and turns it into exile. You should be happy. A pack of blessings lands upon your back; happiness courts you in her best dress, but, like a misbehaving and sullen girl, you frown upon your fortune and your love. Take heed, take heed, for people such as this die miserably. Go to your love, as was decided; climb to her chamber, go and comfort her. But do not stay until the guards are posted, for then you cannot flee to Mantua, where you shall live until we can find a time appropriate to announce your marriage, reconcile your friends, beg the pardon of the Prince, and call you back with a million times more joy than when you left here in sorrow. Go first, Nurse. Commend me to your lady and bid her to urge all in the house to get to bed, which their heavy sorrow makes them likely to do. Romeo is coming.

147

Where thou shalt live till we can find a time
To blaze your marriage, reconcile your friends,
Beg pardon of the Prince, and call thee back
With twenty hundred thousand times more joy
160   Than thou went'st forth in lamentation.
Go before, Nurse. Commend me to thy lady,
And bid her hasten all the house to bed,
Which heavy sorrow makes them apt unto.
Romeo is coming.

165   NURSE: O Lord, I could have stay'd here all the night
To hear good counsel. O, what learning is!
My lord, I'll tell my lady you will come.

ROM: Do so, and bid my sweet prepare to chide.

NURSE: Here is a ring she bid me give you, sir.
170   Hie you, make haste, for it grows very late.   *[Exit.]*

ROM: How well my comfort is reviv'd by this!

FRIAR: Go hence; good night; and here stands all your state:
Either be gone before the watch be set,
Or by the break of day disguis'd from hence.
175   Sojourn in Mantua. I'll find out your man,
And he shall signify from time to time
Every good hap to you that chances here.
Give me thy hand. 'Tis late. Farewell; good night.

ROM: But that a joy past joy calls out on me,
180   It were a grief so brief to part with thee.
Farewell.   *[Exeunt.]*

148

NURSE: Oh, Lord, I could have stayed here all the night to hear such good counsel. Oh, what a joy learning is! My lord, I'll tell my lady you will come.

ROM: Do so, and bid my love to prepare to rebuke me.

NURSE: Here is a ring she bid me give you, sir. Hurry, make haste, for it grows very late.   [Exit.]

ROM: How well my comfort is revived by this!

FRIAR: Go; good night, but remember, this is your situation: either leave before the watch is set, or leave at the break of day in some disguise. Stay in Mantua. I'll find your servant, and he shall tell you from time to time every good news which happens here. Give me your hand. It is late. Farewell; good night.

ROM: If it weren't that a joy beyond joy calls out to me, it would be a grief to part so quickly from you. Farewell.   [Exit.]

SCENE IV
Capulet's House

[Enter Old Capulet, his Wife, and Paris.]

CAP: Things have fall'n out, sir, so unluckily
    That we have had no time to move our daughter.
    Look you, she lov'd her kinsman Tybalt dearly,
    And so did I. Well, we were born to die.
5   'Tis very late; she'll not come down to-night.
    I promise you, but for your company,
    I would have been abed an hour ago.

PAR: These times of woe afford no tune to woo.
    Madam, good night. Commend me to your daughter.

10   LADY: I will, and know her mind early to-morrow;
    To-night she's mew'd up to her heaviness.

CAP: Sir Paris, I will make a desperate tender
    Of my child's love. I think she will be rul'd
    In all respects by me; nay more, I doubt it not.
15   Wife, go you to her ere you go to bed;
    Acquaint her here of my son Paris' love
    And bid her (mark you me?) on Wednesday next—
    But, soft! what day is this?

PAR: Monday, my lord.

20   CAP: Monday! ha, ha! Well, Wednesday is too soon.
    Thursday let it be—a Thursday, tell her
    She shall be married to this noble earl.
    Will you be ready? Do you like this haste?
    We'll keep no great ado—a friend or two;
25   For hark you, Tybalt being slain so late,
    It may be thought we held him carelessly,
    Being our kinsman, if we revel much.
    Therefore we'll have some half a dozen friends,
    And there an end. But what say you to Thursday?

SCENE IV

Capulet's House

[Enter Old Capulet, his Wife, and Paris.]

CAP: *Sir, things have occurred so unluckily that we have had no time to talk with our daughter about your request. You know, she loved her kinsman Tybalt dearly, and so did I. Well, we were all born to die. It is very late; she'll not come down tonight. I tell you that except for your company, I would have been in bed an hour ago.*

PAR: *These times of woe afford no proper chance to woo her. Madam, good night. Give my regards to your daughter.*

LADY: *I will, and you'll know her mind early tomorrow; tonight she's shut up in her sorrows.*

CAP: *Sir Paris, I will make a bold offer of my child's love. I think she will be ruled in all respects by me; truly, I do not doubt it. Wife, go to her before you go to bed; acquaint her with Paris' love and tell her (are you listening?) that on next Wednesday—but, wait! What day is this?*

PAR: *Monday, my lord.*

CAP: *Monday! ha, ha! Well, Wednesday is too soon. Thursday let it be—a Thursday, tell her she shall be married to this noble lord. Will you be ready? Do you like this speed? We'll not have a great gathering—a friend or two only; for as you know, Tybalt was slain recently, and it may be thought that we thought of him carelessly, as he was our kinsman, if we revel too much. Therefore, we'll have some half a dozen friends, and that will be all. But what do you say to Thursday?*

30   PAR: My lord, I would that Thursday were to-morrow.

      CAP: Well, get you gone. A Thursday be it then.
           Go you to Juliet ere you go to bed;
           Prepare her, wife, against this wedding day.
           Farewell, My lord.—Light to my chamber, ho!
35   Afore me, it is so very very late
           That we may call it early by-and-by.
           Good night.   *[Exeunt.]*

SCENE V
Juliet's Chamber.

[Enter Romeo and Juliet aloft, at the Window.]

      JUL: Wilt thou be gone? It is not yet near day.
           It was the nightingale, and not the lark,
           That pierc'd the fearful hollow of thine ear.
           Nightly she sings on yon pomegranate tree.
5   Believe me, love, it was the nightingale.

      ROM: It was the lark, the herald of the morn;
           No nightingale. Look, love, what envious streaks
           Do lace the severing clouds in yonder East.
           Night's candles are burnt out, and jocund day
10   Stands tiptoe on the misty mountain tops.
           I must be gone and live, or stay and die.

      JUL: Yon light is not daylight; I know it, I.
           It is some meteor that the sun exhales
           To be to thee this night a torchbearer
15   And light thee on thy way to Mantua.
           Therefore stay yet; thou need'st not to be gone.

      ROM: Let me be ta'en, let me be put to death.
           I am content, so thou wilt have it so.
           I'll say yon grey is not the morning's eye,

PAR: My lord, I wish that Thursday were tomorrow.

CAP: Well, you should go. Thursday it is then. Go to Juliet before you go to bed; prepare her, wife, for this wedding day. Farewell, my lord. Light up my chamber before me. It is so very, very late that we may call it early morning soon. Good night.   [Exit.]

SCENE V

Juliet's Chamber.

[Enter Romeo and Juliet aloft, at the window.]

JUL: Do you have to go? It is not yet quite day. It was the nightingale and not the morning bird that filled your ear. Nightly she sings on that pomegranate tree. Believe me, love, it was the nightingale.

ROM: It was the lark who calls in the morning, not a nightingale. Look, love, what envious streaks do delicately lay on the clouds far in the East. Night's candles are burned out, and the day happily stands poised on the misty mountain tops. I must be gone and live, or stay and die.

JUL: That far light is not daylight; I know it, I do. It is some meteor that the sun exhales to be a torchbearer for you this night and light your way to Mantua. Therefore, stay awhile; you need not be gone.

ROM: Let me be taken; let me be put to death. I am content if you would have it so. I'll say that grey sky is not the morning's eye, that it is only the pale reflection of the moon's brow; neither is it the lark whose notes beat in the

153

20   'Tis but the pale reflex of Cynthia's brow;
        Nor that is not the lark whose notes do beat
        The vaulty heaven so high above our heads.
        I have more care to stay than will to go.
        Come, death, and welcome! Juliet wills it so.
25   How is't, my soul? Let's talk; it is not day.

JUL: It is, it is! Hie hence, be gone, away!
        It is the lark that sings so out of tune,
        Straining harsh discords and unpleasing sharps.
        Some say the lark makes sweet division;
30   This doth not so, for she divideth us.
        Some say the lark and loathed toad changed eyes;
        O, now I would they had chang'd voices too,
        Since arm from arm that voice doth us affray,
        Hunting thee hence with hunt's-up to the day!
35   O, now be gone! More light and light it grows.

ROM: More light and light—more dark and dark our woes!

[Enter Nurse.]

NURSE: Madam!

JUL: Nurse?

NURSE: Your lady mother is coming to your chamber.
40   The day is broke; be wary, look about.   *[Exit Nurse.]*

JUL: Then, window, let day in, and let life out.

ROM: Farewell, farewell! One kiss, and I'll descend. [He goeth down.]

JUL: Art thou gone so, my lord, my love, my friend?
        I must hear from thee every day in the hour,
45   For in a minute there are many days.
        O, by this count I shall be much in years
        Ere I again behold my Romeo!

154

sky high above our heads. I have more wish to stay than a will to go. Come, death, welcome! Juliet wills it so. How is it, my soul? Let's talk; it is not day.

JUL: It is, it is! Go away; be gone, away! It is indeed the lark that sings so out of tune, straining harsh discords and unpleasant notes. Some say the lark makes sweet music; this is not so, for she divides us. Some say the lark and slimy toad changed eyes; now I wish that they had changed voices, too, since that voice frightens us out of each other's arms, forcing you from here with its morning wake-up call. Oh, go now! It grows more and more light.

ROM: As it gets more light—more dark are our woes!

[Enter Nurse.]

NURSE: Madam!

JUL: Nurse?

NURSE: Your mother is on her way to your chamber. The day is started. Be wary; look about you.   [Exit Nurse.]

JUL: Then, window, let day in, and let life out.

ROM: Farewell, farewell! One kiss, and I'll descend. [He goes down.]

JUL: Are you gone, my lord, my love, my friend? I must hear from you every hour of the day, for every minute you are absent seems like many days. Oh, by this count, I shall be much older before I again behold my Romeo!

ROM: Farewell! I will omit no opportunity
That may convey my greetings, love, to thee.

50 JUL: O, think'st thou we shall ever meet again?

ROM: I doubt it not; and all these woes shall serve
For sweet discourses in our time to come.

JUL: O God, I have an ill-divining soul!
Methinks I see thee, now thou art below,
55 As one dead in the bottom of a tomb.
Either my eyesight fails, or thou look'st pale.

ROM: And trust me, love, in my eye so do you.
Dry sorrow drinks our blood. Adieu, adieu!   [Exit.]

JUL: O Fortune, Fortune! all men call thee fickle.
60 If thou art fickle, what dost thou with him
That is renown'd for faith? Be fickle, Fortune,
For then I hope thou wilt not keep him long
But send him back.

LADY: [Within] Ho, daughter! are you up?

65 JUL: Who is't that calls? It is my lady mother.
Is she not down so late, or up so early?
What unaccustom'd cause procures her hither?

[Enter Lady Capulet.]

LADY: Why, how now, Juliet?

JUL: Madam, I am not well.

70 LADY: Evermore weeping for your cousin's death?
What, wilt thou wash him from his grave with tears?
An if thou could'st, thou could'st not make him live.
Therefore have done. Some grief shows much of love;
But much of grief shows still some want of wit.

ROM: *Farewell! I will miss no chance to convey my greetings, love, to you.*

JUL: *Oh, do you think that we shall ever meet again?*

ROM: *I do not doubt it, and all these woes shall serve for sweet stories in our time to come.*

JUL: *Oh, God, I have a soul that forsees a bad future! I think I see you; now you are below, as one who is dead at the bottom of a tomb. Either my eyesight fails, or you look very pale.*

ROM: *Trust me, love, in my eyes, so do you also. It is only thirsty sorrow that drinks our blood. Good-bye, Good-bye!*   [Exit.]

JUL: *Oh, Fortune, Fortune! All men call you fickle. If you are fickle, what will you do with him who is renowned for his faith? Be fickle, Fortune, for then I hope you will not keep him from me very long, but send him back.*

LADY: [Within.] *Hello, daughter! Are you up?*

JUL: *Who is it that calls me? It is my dear mother. Has she not yet gone to bed or is she up so early? What unusual cause brings her to me?*

[Enter Lady Capulet.]

LADY: *Well, how are you, Juliet?*

JUL: *Madam, I am not well.*

LADY: *Still weeping for your cousin's death? What, will you wash him from his grave with tears? Even if you could, you could not make him live. Anyway, be finished. A little grief shows you loved him greatly, but too much grief shows a lack of understanding.*

75   JUL: Yet let me weep for such a feeling loss.

      LADY: So shall you feel the loss, but not the friend
            Which you weep for.

      JUL: Feeling so the loss,
            I cannot choose but ever weep the friend.

80   LADY: Well, girl, thou weep'st not so much for his death
            As that the villain lives which slaughter'd him.

      JUL: What villain, madam?

      LADY: That same villain Romeo.

      JUL: [Aside.] Villain and he be many miles asunder.
85   God pardon him! I do, with all my heart;
            And yet no man like he doth grieve my heart.

      LADY: That is because the traitor murderer lives.

      JUL: Ay, madam, from the reach of these my hands.
            Would none but I might venge my cousin's death!

90   LADY: We will have vengeance for it, fear thou not.
            Then weep no more. I'll send to one in Mantua,
            Where that same banish'd runagate doth live,
            Shall give him such an unaccustom'd dram
            That he shall soon keep Tybalt company;
95   And then I hope thou wilt be satisfied.

      JUL: Indeed I never shall be satisfied
            With Romeo till I behold him—dead—
            Is my poor heart so for a kinsman vex'd.
            Madam, if you could find out but a man
100   To bear a poison, I would temper it;
            That Romeo should, upon receipt thereof,
            Soon sleep in quiet. O, how my heart abhors
            To hear him nam'd and cannot come to him,
            To wreak the love I bore my cousin Tybalt
105   Upon his body that hath slaughter'd him!

158

JUL: Yet, let me weep for such a feeling of loss.

LADY: You shall feel the loss, but not the friend whom you weep for.

JUL: Feeling this loss so deeply, I cannot choose except to weep for the friend.

LADY: Well, girl, you weep not only because Tybalt is dead, but also because the villain still lives who killed him.

JUL: What villain, madam?

LADY: That same villain Romeo.

JUL: [Aside.] Villain and he are many miles apart.—God pardon him! I do, with all my heart, and yet no other man than he hurts my heart.

LADY: That is because that traitorous murderer lives.

JUL: Ay, madam, far from the reach of my hands. I wish that only I might revenge my cousin's death.

LADY: We will have revenge for it, fear it not. But weep no more. I'll send a message to one in Mantua, where that same banished renegade lives; that person shall give Romeo such a poisoned drink that Romeo will soon join company with dead Tybalt, and then, I hope you will be satisfied.

JUL: Indeed, I will never be satisfied with Romeo until I see him—dead—is my poor heart for a troubled kinsman. Madam, if you could find out such a man to bear that poison, I would temper it, so Romeo should, when he receives it, soon sleep in quiet. My heart hates to hear Romeo named and I cannot come to him, and wreak love I bore my cousin Tybalt upon the body of he who has killed Tybalt!

159

LADY: Find thou the means, and I'll find such a man.
But now I'll tell thee joyful tidings, girl.

JUL: And joy comes well in such a needy time.
What are they, I beseech your ladyship?

110 LADY: Well, well, thou hast a careful father, child;
One who, to put thee from thy heaviness,
Hath sorted out a sudden day of joy
That thou expects not, nor I look'd not for.

JUL: Madam, in happy time! What day is that?

115 LADY: Marry, my child, early next Thursday morn
The gallant, young, and noble gentleman,
The County Paris, at Saint Peter's Church,
Shall happily make thee there a joyful bride.

JUL: Now by Saint Peter's Church, and Peter too,
120 He shall not make me there a joyful bride!
I wonder at this haste, that I must wed
Ere he that should be husband comes to woo.
I pray you tell my lord and father, madam,
I will not marry yet; and when I do, I swear
125 It shall be Romeo, whom you know I hate,
Rather than Paris. These are news indeed!

LADY: Here comes your father. Tell him so yourself,
And see how he will take it at your hands.

[Enter Capulet and Nurse.]

CAP: When the sun sets the air doth drizzle dew,
130 But for the sunset of my brother's son
It rains downright.
How now? a conduit, girl? What, still in tears?
Evermore show'ring? In one little body
Thou counterfeit'st a bark, a sea, a wind:
135 For still thy eyes, which I may call the sea,
Do ebb and flow with tears; the bark thy body is

LADY: If you find the means, then I'll find such a man. But now, I'll tell you happy tidings, girl.

JUL: And joy comes just in the nick of time. What is it, I ask your ladyship?

LADY: Well, well, you have a loving father, child; one who, to lighten your problems, has arranged a sudden day of joy that neither you nor I expected.

JUL: Madam, quickly! What day is it?

LADY: Why, child, early next Thursday morning the gallant, young, and noble gentleman, the County Paris, shall make you a joyful bride at Saint Peter's Church.

JUL: Well, by Saint Peter's Church and St. Peter, too, he shall not make me a joyful bride! I wonder at this haste, that I must wed before he that should be my husband comes to woo me. I ask you to tell my lord and my father, madam, I will not marry yet; and when I do marry, I swear it shall be Romeo, whom you know I hate, rather than Paris. This is indeed news!

LADY: Here comes your father. Tell him so yourself, and see how he reacts.

[Enter Capulet and Nurse.]

CAP: When the sun sets, the air drizzles dew, but for the sunset of my brother's son it rains a downpour. What? A fountain, girl? What, still crying? Forevermore weeping? In one little body you fake a boat, a sea, a wind. Your eyes, which I may call the sea, still ebb and flow with tears; the ship, your body, is sailing in this salt flood; the winds, your sighs, who, fighting with your tears and the tears also with them, without a sudden calm will overcome your tempest-tossed body. Well, wife? Have you told her of our decision?

Sailing in this salt flood; the winds, thy sighs,
Who, raging with thy tears and they with them,
Without a sudden calm will overset
140 Thy tempest-tossed body. How now, wife?
Have you delivered to her our decree?

LADY: Ay, sir; but she will none, she gives you thanks.
I would the fool were married to her grave!

CAP: Soft! take me with you, take me with you, Wife.
145 How? Will she none? Doth she not give us thanks?
Is she not proud? Doth she not count her blest,
Unworthy as she is, that we have wrought
So worthy a gentleman to be her bridegroom?

JUL: Not proud you have, but thankful that you have.
150 Proud can I never be of what I hate,
But thankful even for hate that is meant love.

CAP: How, how, how, how, choplogic? What is this?
'Proud'—and 'I thank you' —and 'I thank you not'—
And yet 'not proud'? Mistress minion you,
155 Thank me no thankings, nor proud me no prouds,
But fettle your fine joints 'gainst Thursday next
To go with Paris to Saint Peter's Church,
Or I will drag thee on a hurdle thither.
Out, you green-sickness carrion! Out, you baggage!
160 You tallow-face!

LADY: Fie, fie! what, are you mad?

JUL: Good father, I beseech you on my knees,
Hear me with patience but to speak a word.

CAP: Hang thee, young baggage! disobedient wretch!
165 I tell thee what—get thee to church a Thursday
Or never after look me in the face.
Speak not, reply not, do not answer me!
My fingers itch. Wife, we scarce thought us blest
That God had lent us but this only child;

LADY: Ay, sir, but she will have none of it; but she gives you thanks. I wish the foolish girl were married to her grave!

CAP: Easy! Explain to me, explain to me, wife. How? Will she not marry? Does she not give us thanks? Is she not proud? Does she not count her blessings that, unworthy as she is, we have arranged so great a gentleman to be her bridegroom?

JUL: I am thankful that you wanted to do this for me, but I cannot be proud of something that I hate, only thankful for what you tried to do.

CAP: What, what's this silly logic? What is this? "Proud"—and "I thank you"—and yet "I thank you not."—and yet "I cannot be proud"? My spoiled miss, thank me no "thanks," proud me no "prouds." You just set your mind to going next Thursday with Paris to Saint Peter's Church, or else I will drag you there on a cart. Out, you sick lump of flesh! Out, you worthless thing! You pale girl!

LADY: Shame, shame! What, are you crazy?

JUL: Good father, I beg you on my knees, hear me with patience, let me speak a word.

CAP: Hang you, young baggage! Disobedient wretch! I tell you what—get to church on Thursday or never look me in the face after that. Speak not, reply not; do not answer me! My fist is ready to strike. Wife, we thought ourselves blessed that God had lent us only this child; but now I see this one is one too many and that we were cursed in having her. Leave her, the worthless creature!

170   But now I see this one is one too much,
       And that we have a curse in having her.
       Out on her, hilding!

       NURSE: God in heaven bless her!
       You are to blame, my lord, to rate her so.

175   CAP: And why, my Lady Wisdom? Hold your tongue,
       Good Prudence. Smatter with your gossips, go!

       NURSE: I speak no treason.

       CAP: O, God-i-god-en!

       NURSE: May not one speak?

180   CAP: Peace, you mumbling fool!
       Utter your gravity o'er a gossip's bowl,
       For here we need it not.

       LADY: You are too hot.

       CAP: God's bread! It makes me mad.
185   Day, night, hour, tide, time, work, play,
       Alone, in company, still my care hath been
       To have her match'd; and having now provided
       A gentleman of princely parentage,
       Of fair demesnes, youthful, and nobly train'd,
190   Stuff'd, as they say, with honourable parts,
       Proportion'd as one's thought would wish a man—
       And then to have a wretched puling fool,
       A whining mammet, in her fortune's tender,
       To answer 'I'll not wed, I cannot love;
195   I am too young, I pray you pardon me'!
       But, an you will not wed, I'll pardon you.
       Graze where you will, you shall not house with me.
       Look to't, think on't; I do not use to jest.
       Thursday is near; lay hand on heart, advise:
200   An you be mine, I'll give you to my friend;
       An you be not, hang, beg, starve, die in the streets,

164

NURSE: *God in heaven bless her! You are wrong, my lord, to rant at her so.*

CAP: *And why, Lady Wisdom? Hold your tongue, Good Prudence. Talk with the other gossips—go!*

NURSE: *I speak no treason.*

CAP: *For God's sake! Good night!*

NURSE: *May I not speak?*

CAP: *Quiet, you mumbling fool! Utter your grave thoughts over a gossip's meal, for here we do not need it.*

LADY: *You are too angry.*

CAP: *God's sacrament! It makes me mad. Day, night, hour, tide, time, work, play, alone, and in company, my only thought has been to get her matched. Having now provided a gentleman of princely parentage, of fair lands, young, and nobly trained, filled, as they say, with honorable parts, proportioned as one would wish for a man—and then to have a wretched, whining fool, a whining doll, when her future is made, she answers, "I'll not wed, I cannot love; I am too young, I ask you to excuse me!" But, if you will not wed, I'll excuse you! Eat where you will, you shall not live with me. Look at it, think on it; I do not say this in jest. Thursday is close; lay hand to your heart, advise. If you are mine, I'll give you to my friend; if you are not, hang, beg, starve, die in the streets; for, by my soul, I'll never acknowledge you as mine, neither will what is mine ever do you any good. Believe it. Think about it. I'll not change my mind.* [Exit.]

165

For, by my soul, I'll ne'er acknowledge thee,
Nor what is mine shall never do thee good.
Trust to't. Bethink you. I'll not be forsworn.   *[Exit.]*

205 JUL: Is there no pity sitting in the clouds
That sees into the bottom of my grief?
O sweet my mother, cast me not away!
Delay this marriage for a month, a week;
Or if you do not, make the bridal bed
210 In that dim monument where Tybalt lies.

LADY: Talk not to me, for I'll not speak a word.
Do as thou wilt, for I have done with thee.   *[Exit.]*

JUL: O God!—O Nurse, how shall this be prevented?
My husband is on earth, my faith in heaven.
215 How shall that faith return again to earth
Unless that husband send it me from heaven
By leaving earth? Comfort me, counsel me.
Alack, alack, that heaven should practise stratagems
Upon so soft a subject as myself!
220 What say'st thou? Hast thou not a word of joy?
Some comfort, Nurse.

NURSE: Faith, here it is.
Romeo is banish'd; and all the world to nothing
That he dares ne'er come back to challenge you;
225 Or if he do, it needs must be by stealth.
Then, since the case so stands as now it doth,
I think it best you married with the County.
O, he's a lovely gentleman!
Romeo's a dishclout to him. An eagle, madam,
230 Hath not so green, so quick, so fair an eye
As Paris hath. Beshrew my very heart,
I think you are happy in this second match,
For it excels your first; or if it did not,
Your first is dead—or 'twere as good he were
235 As living here and you no use of him.

JUL: Speak'st thou this from thy heart?

166

JUL: Is there no pity sitting in the heavens that sees into the bottom of my grief? Oh, sweet mother, do not cast me away! Delay this marriage for a month, a week; or if you do not, you make my bridal bed in that dim monument where Tybalt lies.

LADY: Don't talk to me, for I'll not speak a word in your defense. Do as you will, for I am finished with you.   [Exit.]

JUL: Oh, God!—Oh, Nurse, how can this be prevented? My husband is on earth; my faith, my vows are recorded in heaven. How may I marry again on the earth unless my husband sends it to me from heaven by dying? Comfort me; counsel me. Alas, alas, could heaven devise such tricks on so weak a subject as myself! What do you say? Do you not have a word of joy for me? Some comfort, Nurse.

NURSE: Truthfully, here it is. Romeo is banished, and it's clear to all the world that he dare not come back to claim you; or if he does, it will be in secret. Then, since the case stands as now it does, I think it best you married Paris. Oh, he's a handsome gentleman! Romeo's a dishrag next to him. An eagle, madam, has not as green, quick, or fair an eye as Paris has. Curse my very heart! I think you will be happy in this second match, for it even exceeds your first. Anyway, your first is dead to you—or as good as dead, with you living here and having no contact with him.

JUL: Do you speak this from your heart?

167

Nurse: And from my soul too;
   Else beshrew them both.

Jul: Amen!

240   Nurse: What?

Jul: Well, thou hast comforted me marvellous much.
   Go in; and tell my lady I am gone,
   Having displeas'd my father, to Laurence' cell,
   To make confession and to be absolv'd.

245   Nurse: Marry, I will; and this is wisely done.   *[Exit.]*

Jul: Ancient damnation! O most wicked fiend!
   Is it more sin to wish me thus forsworn,
   Or to dispraise my lord with that same tongue
   Which she hath prais'd him with above compare
250   So many thousand times? Go, counsellor!
   Thou and my bosom henceforth shall be twain.
   I'll to the friar to know his remedy.
   If all else fail, myself have power to die.   *[Exit.]*

NURSE: *And from my soul too; otherwise, curse them both.*

JUL: *Amen!*

NURSE: *What?*

JUL: *Well, you have comforted me marvelously well. Go in and tell my lady that, having displeased my father, I am gone to Laurence's cell to make confession and to be forgiven.*

NURSE: *Yes, I will, and this is wisely done.* [Exit.]

JUL: *Ancient devil! Oh, most wicked feind! Is it more sinful to tell me to break my vows, or to damn my lord with the same tongue which praised him so many thousand times as better than all others? Leave, counselor! You and my heart henceforth will be split forever. I'll go to the friar to know his remedy. If all else fails, I have the power to die.* [Exit.]

ACT IV

SCENE I
Friar Laurence's cell.

[Enter Friar Laurence and County Paris.]

FRIAR: On Thursday, sir? The time is very short.

PAR: My father Capulet will have it so,
  And I am nothing slow to slack his haste.

FRIAR: You say you do not know the lady's mind.
5   Uneven is the course; I like it not.

PAR: Immoderately she weeps for Tybalt's death,
  And therefore have I little talk'd of love;
  For Venus smiles not in a house of tears.
  Now, sir, her father counts it dangerous
10   That she do give her sorrow so much sway,
  And in his wisdom hastes our marriage
  To stop the inundation of her tears,
  Which, too much minded by herself alone,
  May be put from her by society.
15   Now do you know the reason of this haste.

FRIAR: *[Aside.]* I would I knew not why it should be slow'd.
  Look, sir, here comes the lady toward my cell.

[Enter Juliet.]

PAR: Happily met, my lady and my wife!

ACT IV

SCENE I
Friar Laurence's cell.

[Enter Friar Laurence and County Paris.]

FRIAR: On Thursday, sir? The time is very short.

PAR: My father Capulet wants it so, and I have no reason to slow his haste.

FRIAR: You say you do not know the lady's mind. The marriage is not regular;
I do not like it.

PAR: Foolishly she weeps for Tybalt's death, and, therefore, I have not talked of
love, for Venus can't smile in a house of tears. Now, sir, her father considers
it dangerous that she gives her sorrow so much control over her, and in his
wisdom he hastens our marriage to stop the flood of her tears. When alone,
she is consumed by crying, and company may keep her from dwelling on sorrow. Now you know the reason of this haste.

FRIAR: [Aside.] I wish I did not know why it should be slowed. Look, sir, here
comes the lady toward my cell.

[Enter Juliet.]

PAR: I'm happy to see you, my lady and my wife!

JUL: That may be, sir, when I may be a wife.

20   PAR: That may be must be, love, on Thursday next.

JUL: What must be shall be.

FRIAR: That's a certain text.

PAR: Come you to make confession to this father?

JUL: To answer that, I should confess to you.

25   PAR: Do not deny to him that you love me.

JUL: I will confess to you that I love him.

PAR: So will ye, I am sure, that you love me.

JUL: If I do so, it will be of more price,
       Being spoke behind your back, than to your face.

30   PAR: Poor soul, thy face is much abus'd with tears.

JUL: The tears have got small victory by that,
       For it was bad enough before their spite.

PAR: Thou wrong'st it more than tears with that report.

JUL: That is no slander, sir, which is a truth;
35   And what I spake, I spake it to my face.

PAR: Thy face is mine, and thou hast sland'red it.

JUL: It may be so, for it is not mine own.
       Are you at leisure, holy father, now,
       Or shall I come to you at evening mass?

40   FRIAR: My leisure serves me, pensive daughter, now.
       My lord, we must entreat the time alone.

JUL: That may be, sir, when I may be a wife.

PAR: That "may" be will be "must" on next Thursday, love.

JUL: What will be, will certainly be.

FRIAR: That's a certain truth.

PAR: Do you come to make confession to this priest?

JUL: If I answered that, I'd be confessing to you.

PAR: Do not deny to him that you love me.

JUL: I will confess to you that I love him.

PAR: You also will, I am sure, confess that you love me.

JUL: If I do so, it will be worth more spoken behind your back, rather than to your face.

PAR: Poor soul, your face is much abused by tears.

JUL: The tears have won only small victory in that, because it was ugly enough before their work.

PAR: You wrong it with more than tears by that speech.

JUL: There is no slander, sir, in a truth, and what I spoke, I spoke to my own face.

PAR: Your face is mine, and you have abused it.

JUL: That may be true, for it is not my own. Do you have time now, holy father, or should I come to you at evening mass?

FRIAR: My leisure serves me now, sad daughter; my lord, we must spend some time alone.

PAR: God shield I should disturb devotion!
    Juliet, on Thursday early will I rouse ye.
    Till then, adieu, and keep this holy kiss.   *[Exit.]*

45   JUL: O, shut the door! and when thou hast done so,
    Come weep with me—past hope, past cure, past help!

FRIAR: Ah, Juliet, I already know thy grief;
    It strains me past the compass of my wits.
    I hear thou must, and nothing may prorogue it,
50   On Thursday next be married to this County.

JUL: Tell me not, friar, that thou hear'st of this,
    Unless thou tell me how I may prevent it.
    If in thy wisdom thou canst give no help,
    Do thou but call my resolution wise
55   And with this knife I'll help it presently.
    God join'd my heart and Romeo's, thou our hands;
    And ere this hand, by thee to Romeo seal'd,
    Shall be the label to another deed,
    Or my true heart with treacherous revolt
60   Turn to another, this shall slay them both.
    Therefore, out of thy long-experienc'd time,
    Give me some present counsel; or, behold,
    'Twixt my extremes and me this bloody knife
    Shall play the umpire, arbitrating that
65   Which the commission of thy years and art
    Could to no issue of true honour bring.
    Be not so long to speak. I long to die
    If what thou speak'st speak not of remedy.

FRIAR: Hold, daughter. I do spy a kind of hope,
70   Which craves as desperate an execution
    As that is desperate which we would prevent.
    If, rather than to marry County Paris,
    Thou hast the strength of will to slay thyself,
    Then is it likely thou wilt undertake
75   A thing like death to chide away this shame,
    That cop'st with death himself to scape from it;
    And, if thou dar'st, I'll give thee remedy.

PAR: *God forbid that I should disturb such devotion! Juliet, on Thursday I will wake you early. Until then, good-bye, and keep this holy kiss.*   [Exit.]

JUL: *Oh, shut the door! and when you have done it, come weep with me—past hope, past cure, past help!*

FRIAR: *Oh, Juliet, I already know your grief; it strains me past the limits of my wits. I hear that you must next Thursday be married to Paris, and nothing can prevent it.*

JUL: *Don't tell me, friar, that you heard this unless you can tell me how I may prevent it. If, in your wisdom, you can give me no help, then say my plan is wise and with this knife, I'll finish it immediately. God joined my heart with Romeo's; you joined our hands, and before this hand, which sealed my love to Romeo, shall be given to Paris, or my true heart turn to another, this knife shall slay them both. Therefore, using your long years of experience, give me some counsel now, or see how this bloody knife shall play the umpire between my extreme position and me. In that way, I'll solve that which your years and ability could not straighten out honorably. Do not take so long to speak. I long to die if what you speak does not speak of remedy.*

FRIAR: *Wait, daughter. I do spy a kind of hope; it requires a desperation in execution nearly as desperate as what we would prevent. But, if, rather than marry County Paris, you have the strength of will to slay yourself, then it is likely you will undertake a faked death to drive away this shame. If you dare, I'll give you a remedy.*

JUL: O, bid me leap, rather than marry Paris,
From off the battlements of yonder tower,
80   Or walk in thievish ways, or bid me lurk
Where serpents are; chain me with roaring bears,
Or shut me nightly in a charnel house,
O'ercover'd quite with dead men's rattling bones,
With reeky shanks and yellow chapless skulls;
85   Or bid me go into a new-made grave
And hide me with a dead man in his shroud—
Things that, to hear them told, have made me tremble—
And I will do it without fear or doubt,
To live an unstain'd wife to my sweet love.

90 FRIAR: Hold, then. Go home, be merry, give consent
To marry Paris. Wednesday is to-morrow.
To-morrow night look that thou lie alone;
Let not the Nurse lie with thee in thy chamber.
Take thou this vial, being then in bed,
95   And this distilled liquor drink thou off;
When presently through all thy veins shall run
A cold and drowsy humour; for no pulse
Shall keep his native progress, but surcease;
No warmth, no breath, shall testify thou liv'st;
100   The roses in thy lips and cheeks shall fade
To paly ashes, thy eyes' windows fall
Like death when he shuts up the day of life;
Each part, depriv'd of supple government,
Shall, stiff and stark and cold, appear like death;
105   And in this borrowed likeness of shrunk death
Thou shalt continue two-and-forty hours,
And then awake as from a pleasant sleep.
Now, when the bridegroom in the morning comes
To rouse thee from thy bed, there art thou dead.
110   Then, as the manner of our country is,
In thy best robes uncovered on the bier
Thou shalt be borne to that same ancient vault
Where all the kindred of the Capulets lie.
In the mean time, against thou shalt awake,
115   Shall Romeo by my letters know our drift;
And hither shall he come; and he and I

JUL: *Force me to leap off the battlements of that tower, or act in thievish ways; bid me to dwell where serpents are, chain me with roaring bears, or shut me nightly in a tomb, covered with dead men's rattling bones, stinking legs and yellowed jawless skulls. Make me go into a newly made grave and hide me with a dead man in his burial clothing, rather than marry Paris. To hear of such things has previously made me tremble,—yet I will do them without fear or doubt, in order to live like an unstained wife to my sweet love.*

FRIAR: *Wait then. Go home, be happy, give your consent to marrying Paris. Wednesday is tomorrow. Tomorrow night make sure that you lie alone; do not let the Nurse lie with you in your chamber. Take this vial when you are in bed. Drink this distilled liquor, and soon through all your veins shall run a cold and drowsy feeling, for no pulse shall continue its natural progress. Instead, it will cease; no warmth, no breath, shall testify that you live. The roses in your lips and cheeks shall fade to pale ashes; your eyelids will fall like one who is dead. Each part, deprived of supple control, shall, stiff and stark and cold, appear like death, and in this appearance of death, you shall continue forty-two hours and then awaken as if from a pleasant sleep. Now, when the bridegroom in the morning comes to rouse you from your bed, you will appear dead. Then, as is the custom of our country, in your best clothes uncovered on the coffin, you shall be carried to that same ancient vault where all the relatives of the Capulets lie. In the meantime, before you shall wake, Romeo shall know of our plan by my letters, and he shall come here. He and I will watch you wake, and that very night shall Romeo carry you to Mantua. And this shall free you from this present shame if no change or womanish fear stops your valor from acting on this plan.*

Will watch thy waking, and that very night
Shall Romeo bear thee hence to Mantua.
And this shall free thee from this present shame,
120   If no inconstant toy nor womanish fear
Abate thy valour in the acting it.

JUL: Give me, give me! O, tell not me of fear!

FRIAR: Hold! Get you gone, be strong and prosperous
In this resolve. I'll send a friar with speed
125   To Mantua, with my letters to thy lord.

JUL: Love give me strength! and strength shall help afford.
Farewell, dear father.   *[Exeunt.]*

SCENE II

Capulet's House.

[Enter Father Capulet, Lady Capulet, Nurse, and Servingmen, two or three.]

CAP: So many guests invite as here are writ.   *[Exit a Servingman.]*
Sirrah, go hire me twenty cunning cooks.

SERV: You shall have none ill, sir; for I'll try if they can lick their
fingers.

5   CAP: How canst thou try them so?

SERV: Marry, sir, 'tis an ill cook that cannot lick his own fingers.
Therefore he that cannot lick his fingers goes not with me.

CAP: Go, begone.   *[Exit Servingman.]*
We shall be much unfurnish'd for this time.
10   What, is my daughter gone to Friar Laurence?

JUL: *Give it to me; give it to me! Oh, don't talk to me of fear!*

FRIAR: *Leave quickly; be strong and prosperous in this resolve. I'll send a friar quickly to Mantua with my letters to your lord.*

JUL: *Love give me strength! And strength shall help put it into practice. Farewell, dear father.* [Exit.]

SCENE II
Capulet's House.

[Enter Father Capulet, Lady Capulet, Nurse, and Servingmen, two or three.]

CAP: *Invite as many guests as are written on this list.* [Exit a Servingman.] *Sir, go hire twenty brilliant cooks.*

SERV: *You shall not have poor ones, sir, for I'll see if they will lick their fingers.*

CAP: *Why would you test them so?*

SERV: *Well, sir, it is a poor cook that will not lick his own fingers. Therefore, he that will not lick his fingers does not go with me.*

CAP: *Go, be gone.* [Exit Servingman.] *We shall be very unprepared for this time. What, has my daughter gone to Friar Laurence?*

NURSE: Ay, forsooth.

CAP: Well, be may chance to do some good on her.
    A peevish self-will'd harlotry it is.

[Enter Juliet.]

NURSE: See where she comes from shrift with merry
15   look.

CAP: How now, my headstrong? Where have you been gadding?

JUL: Where I have learnt me to repent the sin
    Of disobedient opposition
    To you and your behests, and am enjoin'd
20   By holy Laurence to fall prostrate here
    To beg your pardon. Pardon, I beseech you!
    Henceforward I am ever rul'd by you.

CAP: Send for the County. Go tell him of this.
    I'll have this knot knit up to-morrow morning.

25   JUL: I met the youthful lord at Laurence' cell
    And gave him what becomed love I might,
    Not stepping o'er the bounds of modesty.

CAP: Why, I am glad on't. This is well. Stand up.
    This is as't should be. Let me see the County.
30   Ay, marry, go, I say, and fetch him hither.
    Now, afore God, this reverend holy friar,
    All our whole city is much bound to him.

JUL: Nurse, will you go with me into my closet
    To help me sort such needful ornaments
35   As you think fit to furnish me to-morrow?

LADY CAP: No, not till Thursday. There is time enough.

CAP: Go, Nurse, go with her. We'll to church to-morrow.
                  [Exeunt Juliet and Nurse.]

180

NURSE: Ay, truly.

CAP: Well, it may chance to do some good for her. A peevish, self-willed girl she is.

[Enter Juliet.]

NURSE: Here she comes from confession with a merry look.

CAP: Hello, my headstrong girl? Where have you been visiting?

JUL: Where I have learned to repent the sin of disobedient opposition to you and your requests, and I am told by holy Laurence to fall at your feet to beg your pardon. Pardon me, I beg you! From now on, I will be ruled by you.

CAP: Send for Paris. Go tell him of this. I'll have this marriage performed tomorrow morning.

JUL: I met the youthful lord at Laurence' cell and gave him what love I might, without stepping over the bounds of modesty.

CAP: Why, I am glad on it. This is well. Stand up. This is as it should be. Let me see Paris. Ay, yes, go, I say, and fetch him here. Now, before God, this reverend holy friar, all our whole city owes much to him.

JUL: Nurse, will you go with me into my room to help me sort such needed accessories as you think fit to furnish me for tomorrow?

LADY CAP: No, not till Thursday. There is time enough.

CAP: Go, Nurse, go with her. We'll go to church tomorrow.

[Exit Juliet and Nurse.]

Lady Cap: We shall be short in our provision.
    'Tis now near night.

40   Cap: Tush, I will stir about,
    And all things shall be well, I warrant thee, wife.
    Go thou to Juliet, help to deck up her.
    I'll not to bed to-night; let me alone.
    I'll play the housewife for this once. What, ho!
45   They are all forth; well, I will walk myself
    To County Paris, to prepare him up
    Against to-morrow. My heart is wondrous light,
    Since this same wayward girl is so reclaim'd.   *[Exeunt.]*

SCENE III
Juliet's Chamber.

[Enter Juliet and Nurse.]

Jul: Ay, those attires are best; but, gentle Nurse,
    I pray thee leave me to myself to-night;
    For I have need of many orisons
    To move the heavens to smile upon my state,
5   Which, well thou knowest, is cross and full of sin.

[Enter Lady Cap.]

Lady Cap: What, are you busy, ho? Need you my help?

Jul: No, madam; we have cull'd such necessaries
    As are behoveful for our state to-morrow.
    So please you, let me now be left alone,
10   And let the Nurse this night sit up with you;
    For I am sure you have your hands full all
    In this so sudden business.

Lady Cap: Good night.
    Get thee to bed, and rest; for thou hast need.
      [Exeunt Lady Capulet and Nurse.]

182

LADY CAP: *We shall be short in our preparations. It is nearly night now.*

CAP: *Well, I will move quickly, and all things shall be well, I promise you, wife. Go to Juliet; help to fix her up. I'll not go to bed tonight; leave me alone. I'll play the housewife for this once. What! They are all gone; well, I will walk myself to County Paris to prepare him for tomorrow. My heart is wondrously light since this same wayward girl is now reclaimed.* [Exit.]

SCENE III
Juliet's Chamber.

[Enter Juliet and Nurse.]

JUL: *Ay, those clothes are the best; but, gentle Nurse, I pray you, leave me to myself tonight. I have need of many prayers to move the heavens to smile upon my being, which, as you know well, is cross and full of sin.*

[Enter Lady Cap.]

LADY CAP: *What, are you still busy? Do you need my help?*

JUL: *No, madam; we have pulled together such necessities as are beneficial for our state tomorrow. So, if you please, let me now be left alone, and let the Nurse sit up this night with you, for I am sure you have your hands all full in this sudden business.*

LADY CAP: *Good night. Get to bed, and rest, for you have need of it.*
[Exit Lady Capulet and Nurse.]

183

15   Jul: Farewell! God knows when we shall meet again.
I have a faint cold fear thrills through my veins
That almost freezes up the heat of life.
I'll call them back again to comfort me.
Nurse!—What should she do here?
20   My dismal scene I needs must act alone.
Come, vial.
What if this mixture do not work at all?
Shall I be married then to-morrow morning?
No, No! This shall forbid it. Lie thou there.
[Lays down a dagger.]
25   What if it be a poison which the friar
Subtilly hath ministr'd to have me dead,
Lest in this marriage he should be dishonour'd
Because he married me before to Romeo?
I fear it is; and yet methinks it should not,
30   For he hath still been tried a holy man.
I will not entertain so bad a thought.
How if, when I am laid into the tomb,
I wake before the time that Romeo
Come to redeem me? There's a fearful point!
35   Shall I not then be stifled in the vault,
To whose foul mouth no healthsome air breathes in,
And there die strangled ere my Romeo comes?
Or, if I live, is it not very like
The horrible conceit of death and night,
40   Together with the terror of the place—
As in a vault, an ancient receptacle
Where for this many hundred years the bones
Of all my buried ancestors are pack'd;
Where bloody Tybalt, yet but green in earth,
45   Lies fest'ring in his shroud; where, as they say,
At some hours in the night spirits resort—
Alack, alack, is it not like that I,
So early waking—what with loathsome smells,
And shrieks like mandrakes torn out of the earth,
50   That living mortals, hearing them, run mad—
O, if I wake, shall I not be distraught,
Environed with all these hideous fears,
And madly play with my forefathers' joints,

184

Jul: *Farewell! God knows when we shall meet again. I have a weak cold fear that runs through my veins and almost freezes up the heat of my life. I'll call them back again to comfort me. Nurse!—What should she do here? My dismal scene needs to be acted alone. Come, vial. What if this mixture does not work at all? Shall I be married then tomorrow morning? No, No! This shall stop it. Lie you there.*

[Lays down a dagger.]

What if it is a poison which the friar has subtly given to me in order to really have me dead, since in marrying me to Paris he would be dishonored because he married me to Romeo before? I fear it is so, and yet I think it should not be so, for he has always been thought a holy man. I will not entertain so wicked a thought. How if, when I am laid into the tomb, I wake before the time that Romeo comes to redeem me? There's a fearful idea! Shall I not then be suffocated in the vault, in whose foul mouth no healthy air is breathed, and there die strangled before my Romeo comes? Or, if I live, isn't it likely that these horrible thoughts of death and night, together with the terror of the place—as in a vault, an ancient tomb where, for this many hundred years, the bones of all my buried ancestors are packed, where bloody Tybalt, only new to the grave, lies rotting in his shroud, where, as they say, at some hours in the night spirits arise? Woe, woe, is it not likely that I, waking early—among these loathsome smells and shrieks that make living mortals, when hearing them, run mad? If I wake, shall I not be distraught, enclosed with all these hideous fears, and play madly with my forefathers' bones and pluck the mangled Tybalt from his shroud and, in this rage, use some great kinsman's bone as a club to dash out my desperate brains? Oh, look! I think I see my cousin's ghost seeking out Romeo, who pierced his body with a rapier. Stop, Tybalt, stop! Romeo, I come! I do drink this to you.

[She drinks and falls upon her bed behind the curtains.]

185

And pluck the mangled Tybalt from his shroud,
55   And, in this rage, with some great kinsman's bone
As with a club dash out my desp'rate brains?
O, look! methinks I see my cousin's ghost
Seeking out Romeo, that did spit his body
Upon a rapier's point. Stay, Tybalt, stay!
60   Romeo, I come! this do I drink to thee.

[She drinks and falls upon her bed within the curtains.]

SCENE IV
Capulet's House.

[Enter Lady Capulet and Nurse.]

LADY: Hold, take these keys and fetch more spices, Nurse.

NURSE: They call for dates and quinces in the pastry.

[Enter Capulet.]

CAP: Come, stir, stir, stir! The second cock hath crow'd,
      The curfew bell hath rung, 'tis three o'clock.
5   Look to the bak'd meats, good Angelica;
      Spare not for cost.

NURSE: Go, you cot-quean, go,
      Get you to bed! Faith, you'll be sick to-morrow
      For this night's watching.

10   CAP: No, not a whit. What, I have watch'd ere now
      All night for lesser cause, and ne'er been sick.

LADY: Ay, you have been a mouse-hunt in your time;
      But I will watch you from such watching now.
                   [Exeunt Lady and Nurse.]

SCENE IV
Capulet's House.

[Enter Lady Capulet and Nurse.]

LADY: Nurse, take these keys and fetch more spices.

NURSE: They call for dates and quinces in the pastry room.

[Enter Capulet.]

CAP: Come, move, move! The second cock has crowed, the curfew bell has rung; it is three o'clock. Look after the baked meats, good Angelica; do not spare any cost.

NURSE: Go, you act like a housewife; go, get to bed! Indeed, you'll be sick tomorrow because of this night's watching.

CAP: No, not a bit. I have watched all night before for smaller reasons and have never been sick.

LADY: Ay, you have been a woman-chaser in your time, but I will stop you from such things now.   [Exit Lady and Nurse.]

CAP: A jealous hood, a jealous hood!
15   Now, fellow, what's thare?

[Enter three or four servingmen, with spits and logs and baskets.]

FIRST SERVANT: Things for the cook, sir; but I know not what.

CAP: Make haste, make haste.   *[Exit First Servant.]*
    Sirrah, fetch drier logs.
    Call Peter; he will show thee where they are.

20   SECOND SERVANT: I have a head, sir, that will find out logs
    And never trouble Peter for the matter. *[Exit Second Servant.]*

CAP: Mass, and well said; a merry whoreson, ha!
    Thou shalt be loggerhead. Good faith, 'tis day.
    The County will be here with music straight,
25   For so he said he would. *[Play of music.]*
    I hear him near.
    Nurse! Wife! What, ho! What, Nurse, I say!

[Enter Nurse.]
    Go waken Juliet; go and trim her up.
    I'll go and chat with Paris. Hie, make haste,
30   Make haste! The bridegroom he is come already:
    Make haste, I say.   *[Exeunt.]*

CAP: A jealous wife, a jealous wife!
  What is it now, man?

[Enter three or four servingmen, with spits of meat and logs and baskets.]

FIRST SERVANT: Things for the cook, sir, but I don't know what.

CAP: Make haste, make haste. [Exit First Servant.] Sir, fetch drier logs. Call
  Peter; he will show you where they are.

SECOND SERVANT: I have a good head, sir, that can find logs easily and have no
  need to trouble Peter for the matter.   [Exit Second Servant.]

CAP: Good, and well said; a merry man, ha! You shall be a blockhead.
  Goodness, it is day. Paris said he would be here with music straight away.
  [Playing of music.]
  I hear him nearby. Nurse! Wife! What, hello! What, Nurse, I say!

[Enter Nurse.]
  Go waken Juliet; help her to get ready. I'll go and chat with Paris. Get going,
  make haste, make haste! The bridegroom has come here already. Make haste,
  I say.   [Exit.]

SCENE V
Juliet's Chamber.

[Enter Nurse.]

NURSE: Mistress! what, mistress! Juliet! Fast, I warrant her, she.
　　Why, lamb! why, lady! Fie, you slug-abed!
　　Why, love, I say! madam! sweetheart! Why, bride!
　　What, not a word? You take your pennyworths now!
5　　Sleep for a week; for the next night, I warrant,
　　The County Paris hath set up his rest
　　That you shall rest but little. God forgive me!
　　Marry, and amen. How sound is she asleep!
　　I needs must wake her. Madam, madam, madam!
10　Ay, let the County take you in your bed!
　　He'll fright you up, i' faith. Will it not be?
[Draws aside the curtains.]
　　What, dress'd, and in your clothes, and down again?
　　I must needs wake you. Lady! lady! lady!
　　Alas, alas! Help, help! My lady's dead!
15　O well-a-day that ever I was born!
　　Some aqua-vitae, ho! My lord! my lady!

[Enter Lady Capulet.]

LADY CAP: What noise is here?

NURSE: O lamentable day!

LADY CAP: What is the matter?

20　NURSE: Look, look! O heavy day!

LADY CAP: O me, O me! My child, my only life!
　　Revive, look up, or I will die with thee!
　　Help, help! Call help.

[Enter Capulet.]

SCENE V
Juliet's Chamber.

[Enter Nurse.]

NURSE: Mistress! What, mistress! Juliet! I believe she is fast asleep. Why, lamb!
why, lady! Shame, you sluggish girl! Why, love, I say! Madam! Sweetheart!
Why, bride! What, not a word? You take your little nap now!
Sleep for a week; for the next night, I promise, the County Paris has set up
his agenda that you shall rest very little. God forgive me! (Good, and amen.)
How sound asleep she is! I need to wake her. Madam, madam, madam! Ay,
let Paris take you in your bed! He'll frighten you awake, for sure. Will it not
be so?

[Draws aside the curtains.]
What, did you get up, dress in your clothes, and lie down again? I must wake
you. Lady! Lady! Lady! Alas, alas! Help, help! My lady's dead! Oh, God, that
I were ever born! Some wine, quick! My lord! my lady!

[Enter Lady Capulet.]

LADY CAPULET: What noise is here?

NURSE: Oh, lamentable day!

LADY CAPULET: What is the matter?

NURSE: Look, look! Oh heavy day!

LADY CAPULET: Oh, me, Oh, me! My child, my only life! Revive, look up, or I will
die with you! Help, help! Call help.

[Enter Capulet.]

CAP: For shame, bring Juliet forth; her lord is come.

25　NURSE: She's dead, deceas'd; she's dead! Alack the day!

LADY CAP: Alack the day, she's dead, she's dead, she's
　　　dead!

CAP: Ha! let me see her. Out alas! she's cold,
　　　Her blood is settled, and her joints are stiff;
30　　　Life and these lips have long been separated.
　　　Death lies on her like an untimely frost
　　　Upon the sweetest flower of all the field.

NURSE: O lamentable day!

LADY CAP: O woful time!

35　CAP: Death, that hath ta'en her hence to make me wail,
　　　Ties up my tongue and will not let me speak.

[Enter Friar Laurence and the County (Paris), with Musicians.]

FRIAR: Come, is the bride ready to go to church?

CAP: Ready to go, but never to return.
　　　O son, the night before thy wedding day
40　　　Hath Death lain with thy wife. See, there she lies,
　　　Flower as she was, deflowered by him.
　　　Death is my son-in-law, Death is my heir;
　　　My daughter he hath wedded. I will die
　　　And leave him all. Life, living, all is Death's.

45　PAR: Have I thought long to see this morning's face,
　　　And doth it give me such a sight as this?

LADY CAPULET: Accurs'd, unhappy, wretched, hateful day!
　　　Most miserable hour that e'er time saw
　　　In lasting labour of his pilgrimage!
50　　　But one, poor one, one poor and loving child,
　　　But one thing to rejoice and solace in,
　　　And cruel Death hath catch'd it from my sight!

192

CAP: *For shame, bring Juliet forth; Paris has come.*

NURSE: *She's dead, deceased; she's dead! Woe is the day!*

LADY CAPULET: *Woe is the day, she's dead, she's dead, she's dead!*

CAP: *Ah! let me see her. Dead, alas! She's cold, her blood has settled, and her joints are stiff; life and these lips have long been separated. Death lies on her like an untimely frost upon the sweetest flower of all the field.*

NURSE: *Oh, lamentable day!*

LADY CAPULET: *Oh, woeful time!*

CAP: *Death that has taken her away to make me cry, ties up my tongue and will not let me speak.*

[Enter Friar Laurence and the County Paris, with Musicians.]

FRIAR: *Come, is the bride ready to go to church?*

CAP: *Ready to go, but never to return.* [To Paris] *Oh, son, the night before your wedding day, death has lain with your wife. See, there she lies, flower as she was, taken by him. Death is my son-in-law, death is my heir; he has wedded my daughter. I will die and leave all to him. Life, living, in the end, all is Death's.*

PAR: *I have long looked forward to this morning's face, and now it gives me such a sight as this?*

LADY CAPULET: *Accursed, unhappy, wretched, hateful day! This is a most miserable hour. To have but one, one poor, one poor and loving child, the one thing to rejoice and feel good in, and now cruel Death has snatched her from my sight!*

193

NURSE: O woe! O woeful, woeful, woeful day!
　　　Most lamentable day, most woeful day
55　　That ever ever I did yet behold!
　　　O day! O day! O day! O hateful day!
　　　Never was seen so black a day as this.
　　　O woeful day! O woful day!

PAR: Beguil'd, divorced, wronged, spited, slain!
60　　Most detestable Death, by thee beguil'd
　　　By cruel cruel thee quite overthrown!
　　　O love! O life! not life, but love in death!

CAP: Despis'd, distressed, hated, martyr'd, kill'd!
　　　Uncomfortable time, why cam'st thou now
65　　To murder, murder our solemnity?
　　　O child! O child! my soul, and not my child!
　　　Dead art thou, dead! alack, my child is dead,
　　　And with my child my joys are buried!

FRIAR: Peace, ho, for shame! Confusion's cure lives not
70　　In these confusions. Heaven and yourself
　　　Had part in this fair maid! now heaven hath all,
　　　And all the better is it for the maid.
　　　Your part in her you could not keep from death,
　　　But heaven keeps his part in eternal life.
75　　The most you sought was her promotion,
　　　For 'twas your heaven she should be advanc'd;
　　　And weep ye now, seeing she is advanc'd
　　　Above the clouds, as high as heaven itself?
　　　O, in this love, you love your child so ill
80　　That you run mad, seeing that she is well.
　　　She's not well married that lives married long,
　　　But she's best married that dies married young.
　　　Dry up your tears and stick your rosemary
　　　On this fair corse, and, as the custom is,
85　　In all her best array bear her to church;
　　　For though fond nature bids us all lament,
　　　Yet nature's tears are reason's merriment.

NURSE: *Oh, woe! Oh, woeful, woeful, woeful day! Most lamentable day, most woeful day that I ever beheld! Oh, day! Oh, day! Oh, day! Oh, hateful day! Never was seen so black a day as this. Oh, woeful day! Oh, woeful day!*

PAR: *I have been tricked, divorced, wronged, spited, slain! Most detestable Death, by your trickery, by cruel cruelty you have quite destroyed me! Oh, love! Oh, life! Not life, but love in death!*

CAP: *Despised, distressed, hated, martyred, killed! Time without comfort, why did you come now to murder our festivities? Oh, child! Oh, child! Not just my child, but also my soul! Dead you are, dead! Alas, my child is dead, and with my child, my joys are also buried!*

FRIAR: *Peace, now, for shame! The cure for this confusion doesn't live in this chaos. Heaven and yourself had shared this fair maid! Now heaven has all, and all the better is it for my daughter. Your part of her, you could not keep from death, but heaven keeps his part in eternal life. The most you sought was her promotion to heaven, for it was your heaven she should be moving towards; now you weep, seeing that she is moving above the clouds, as high as heaven itself? Oh, in this love, you love your child so poorly that you run mad, seeing that she is really well. She is not well married who lives a long married life, but she who is married best dies married young. Dry up your tears and stick your fragrant herbs on this fair corpse, and, as is customary, carry her to church in all her best clothes. Though our loving natures bid us all feel sadness, reason laughs at our tears.*

195

CAP: All things that we ordained festival
     Turn from their office to black funeral—
90   Our instruments to melancholy bells,
     Our wedding cheer to a sad burial feast;
     Our solemn hymns to sullen dirges change;
     Our bridal flowers serve for a buried corse;
     And all things change them to the contrary.

95   FRIAR: Sir, go you in; and, madam, go with him;
     And go, Sir Paris. Every one prepare
     To follow this fair corse unto her grave.
     The heavens do low'r upon you for some ill;
     Move them no more by crossing their high will.
100   *[Exeunt. Capulet, Lady Capulet, Paris,and Friar.]*

1. MUS: Faith, we may put up our pipes and be gone.

NURSE: Honest good fellows, ah, put up, put up!
     For well you know this is a pitiful case.   *[Exit Nurse.]*

1. MUS: Ay, by my troth, the case may be amended.

[Enter Peter.]

105 PET: Musicians, O, musicians, 'Heart's ease, Heart's ease'! O, an you
     will have me live, play 'Heart's ease.'

1. MUS: Why 'Heart's ease'?

PET: O, musicians, because my heart itself plays 'My heart is full of
     woe.' O, play me some merry dump to comfort me.

110 1. MUS Not a dump we! 'Tis no time to play now.

PET: You will not then?

1. MUS: No.

PET: I will then give it you soundly.

196

CAP: *All things that we had here for the festival will now be used for a black funeral—our instruments turned to melancholy bells, our wedding cheer to a sad burial feast, our solemn hymns to somber songs. Our bridal flowers serve for a buried corpse, and all things change themselves to the opposite.*

FRIAR: *Sir, go in; and, madam, go with him; and go, Sir Paris. Every one prepare to follow this fair corpse to her grave. The heavens do lower upon you some evil; do not anger them more by crossing their high will.*

[Exit Capulet, Lady Capulet, Paris, and Friar.]

1. MUS: *Indeed, we may put away our pipes and be gone.*

NURSE: *Honest good fellows, ah, put them away, put them away! For well you see this is a pitiful occasion.*   [Exit Nurse.]

1. MUS: *Ay, by my truth, the case may be fixed.*

[Enter Peter.]

PET: *Musicians, musicians, play "Heart's ease," "Heart's ease"! If you wish me to live, play "Heart's ease."*

1. MUS: *Why "Heart's ease"?*

PET: *Oh, musicians, because my heart itself plays "My heart is full of woe." Oh, play me some merry song to comfort me.*

1. MUS: *Not us, no song! It is no time to play now.*

PET: *You will not then?*

1. MUS: *No.*

PET: *I will then give it to you soundly.*

1. MUS: What will you give us?

115 PET: No money, on my faith, but the gleek. I will give you the
   minstrel.

1. MUS: Then will I give you the serving-creature.

PET: Then will I lay the serving-creature's dagger on your pate. I will carry no
   crotchets. I'll re you, I'll fa you.
120   Do you note me?

1. MUS: An you re us and fa us, you note us.

2. MUS: Pray you put up your dagger, and put out your wit.

PET: Then have at you with my wit! I will dry-beat you with an iron
   wit, and put up my iron dagger. Answer me like men.

125   'When griping grief the heart doth wound,
     And doleful dumps the mind oppress,
     Then music with her silver sound'—

     Why 'silver sound'? Why 'music with her silver sound'?
     What say you, Simon Catling?

130 1. MUS Marry, sir, because silver hath a sweet sound.

PET: Pretty! What say you, Hugh Rebeck?

2. MUS: I say 'silver sound' because musicians sound for silver.

PET: Pretty too! What say you, James Soundpost?

3. MUS: Faith, I know not what to say.

135 PET: O, I cry you mercy! you are the singer. I will say for you. It is
   'music with her silver sound' because musicians have no gold for
   sounding.

1. MUS: *What will you give us?*

PET: *No money, on my honor, only a jest. I will turn you out like a minstrel.*

1. MUS: *Then I will treat you like a serving-creature.*

PET: *Then I will lay the serving-creature's dagger on your head. I will carry no tunes. I'll "re" you, I'll "fa" you. Do you note me?*

1. MUS: *If you "re" us and "fa" us, you note us.*

2. MUS: *I pray you, put away your dagger, and pull out your wits.*

PET: *Then I'll have at you with my wit! I will beat you with a strong wit and put away my iron dagger. Answer me like men.*

> *"When griping grief wounds the heart,*
> *And crushing woe oppresses the mind,*
> *Then music with her silvery sound"—*

Why "silvery sound"? Why "music with her silvery sound"? What do you think, Simon Catgut?

1. MUS: *Only, sir, because silver has a sweet sound.*

PET: *Pretty! What do you say, Hugh Echo?*

2. MUS: *I say "silver sound" because musicians play for silver.*

PET: *Good answer too! What do you say, James Soundingboard?*

3. MUS: *In truth, I don't know what to say.*

PET: *Oh, I beg your pardon! You are merely the singer. I will "say" it for you. It is "music with her silvery sound" because musicians get no gold for playing.*

199

'Then music with her silver sound
With speedy help doth lend redress.'   [Exit.]

140   1. MUS: What a pestilent knave is this same!

2. MUS: Hang him, Jack! Come, we'll in here, tarry for the mourners,
and stay dinner.
                                                [Exeunt.]

"Then music with her silvery sound
With speedy help does lend aid."   [Exit.]

1. Mus: What an obnoxious dunce he is!

2. Mus: Hang him, Jack! Come, we'll go in here; we'll wait for the mourners, and stay for dinner.   [Exit.]

ACT V

SCENE I
Mantua. A street.

[Enter Romeo.]

Rom: If I may trust the flattering truth of sleep,
My dreams presage some joyful news at hand.
My bosom's lord sits lightly in his throne,
And all this day an unaccustom'd spirit
5   Lifts me above the ground with cheerful thoughts.
I dreamt my lady came and found me dead
(Strange dream that gives a dead man leave to think!)
And breath'd such life with kisses in my lips
That I reviv'd and was an emperor.
10   Ah me! how sweet is love itself possess'd,
When but love's shadows are so rich in joy!

[Enter Romeo's man Balthasar, booted.]
News from Verona! How now, Balthasar?
Dost thou not bring me letters from the friar?
How doth my lady? Is my father well?
15   How fares my Juliet? That I ask again,
For nothing can be ill if she be well.

Bal: Then she is well, and nothing can be ill.
Her body sleeps in Capels' monument,
And her immortal part with angels lives.
20   I saw her laid low in her kindred's vault
And presently took post to tell it you.
O, pardon me for bringing these ill news,
Since you did leave it for my office, sir.

ACT V.

SCENE I
Mantua. A street.

[Enter Romeo.]

ROM: *If I may trust the flattering pictures of sleep, my dreams predict some joyful news is coming soon. My love sits lightly in my heart, and all this day, an unaccustomed spirit lifts me above the ground with cheerful thoughts. I dreamed that my lady came and found me dead (It is a strange dream that gives a dead man permission to think!). She then breathed life with her kisses into my lips, and I revived and was a king. Ah, me! How sweet is love when it is returned, and when love's fancies are so rich in joy!*

[Enter Romeo's man, Balthasar, with boots on.]
News from Verona! Well, Balthasar? Do you not bring me letters from the friar? How does my lady? Is my father well? How is my Juliet? I ask that again, for nothing can be ill if she is well.

BAL: *Then she is well, and nothing can be ill. Her body sleeps in the Capulets' tomb, and her immortal soul lies with the angels. I saw her laid low in her family's vault and quickly sped to tell the news to you. Pardon me for bringing this bad news, since you did say it was my duty, sir.*

ROM: Is it e'en so? Then I defy you, stars!
25   Thou knowest my lodging. Get me ink and paper
      And hire posthorses. I will hence to-night.

BAL: I do beseech you, sir, have patience.
     Your looks are pale and wild and do import
     Some misadventure.

30   ROM: Tush, thou art deceiv'd.
     Leave me and do the thing I bid thee do.
     Hast thou no letters to me from the friar?

BAL: No, my good lord.

ROM: No matter. Get thee gone
35   And hire those horses. I'll be with thee straight. *[Exit Balthasar.]*
      Well, Juliet, I will lie with thee to-night.
      Let's see for means. O mischief, thou art swift
      To enter in the thoughts of desperate men!
      I do remember an apothecary,
40   And hereabouts he dwells, which late I noted
      In tatt'red weeds, with overwhelming brows,
      Culling of simples. Meagre were his looks,
      Sharp misery had worn him to the bones;
      And in his needy shop a tortoise hung,
45   An alligator stuff'd, and other skins
      Of ill-shaped fishes; and about his shelves
      A beggarly account of empty boxes,
      Green earthen pots, bladders, and musty seeds,
      Remnants of packthread, and old cakes of roses
50   Were thinly scattered, to make up a show.
      Noting this penury, to myself I said,
      'An if a man did need a poison now
      Whose sale is present death in Mantua,
      Here lives a caitiff wretch would sell it him.'
55   O, this same thought did but forerun my need,
      And this same needy man must sell it me.
      As I remember, this should be the house.
      Being holiday, the beggar's shop is shut.
      What, ho! apothecary!

ROM: Is it true? Then I defy you, fate! You know my lodging. [To servant] *Get me ink and paper and hire horses. I will go there tonight.*

BAL: I do beseech you, sir, have patience. Your looks are pale and wild and do suggest some danger.

ROM: No, you are deceived. Leave me and do the thing I bid you do. Have you no letters for me from the friar?

BAL: No, my good lord.

ROM: No matter. Leave and hire those horses. I'll be with you straightaway.
[Exit Balthasar.]

Well, Juliet, I will lie with you tonight. Let's see how it can be done. Oh, mischief, you are swift to enter into the thoughts of desperate men! I remember a pharmacist who dwells around here, who I recently noted wears tattered clothes, is ill-kempt, and gathers herbs. His looks are so thin, as if painful misery had worn him to the bones, and in his meager shop hung a tortoise, a stuffed alligator, and other skins of ill-shaped fishes. On his shelves are a great number of empty boxes, green earthen pots, bladders, and musty seeds; remnants of string, and old pressed roses were thinly scattered to make up a display. Noting this poverty, I said to myself, "If a man needed a poison whose sale is at present forbidden in Mantua, here lives a slave who would sell it to him." Oh, this same thought occurred to me only shortly before my need of him, and this same needy man must sell it to me. As I remember, this should be the house. Being a holiday, the beggar's shop is shut. What, hello! Pharmacist!

[Enter Apothecary.]

60   APOTH: Who calls so loud?

        ROM: Come hither, man. I see that thou art poor.
            Hold, there is forty ducats. Let me have
            A dram of poison, such soon-speeding gear
            As will disperse itself through all the veins
65   That the life-weary taker may fall dead,
            And that the trunk may be discharg'd of breath
            As violently as hasty powder fir'd
            Doth hurry from the fatal cannon's womb.

        APOTH: Such mortal drugs I have; but Mantua's law
70   Is death to any he that utters them.

        ROM: Art thou so bare and full of wretchedness
            And fearest to die? Famine is in thy cheeks,
            Need and oppression starveth in thine eyes,
            Contempt and beggary hangs upon thy back:
75   The world is not thy friend, nor the world's law;
            The world affords no law to make thee rich;
            Then be not poor, but break it and take this.

        APOTH: My poverty but not my will consents.

        ROM: I pay thy poverty and not thy will.

80   APOTH: Put this in any liquid thing you will
            And drink it off, and if you had the strength
            Of twenty men, it would dispatch you straight.

        ROM: There is thy gold—worse poison to men's souls,
            Doing more murderer in this loathsome world,
85   Than these poor compounds that thou mayst not sell.
            I sell thee poison; thou hast sold me none.
            Farewell. Buy food and get thyself in flesh.
            Come, cordial and not poison, go with me
            To Juliet's grave; for there must I use thee.   *[Exeunt.]*

[Enter Apothecary.]

APOTH: *Who calls so loudly?*

ROM: *Come here, man. I see that you are poor. Here are forty gold coins. Let me have a portion of poison, some quick-acting brew that will disperse itself through all veins so that a life-weary person might fall dead and have his body emptied of breath as quickly as powder fired from a fatal cannon.*

APOTH: *I have such fatal drugs, but Mantua's law says death to any that sell them.*

ROM: *Do you, who is so hungry and full of wretchedness, fear death? Famine is in your cheeks; need and oppression is seen in your eyes; contempt and poverty hang upon your back. The world is not your friend, nor is the world's law; the world has no law to make you rich; then be not poor, but break the law and take this gold.*

APOTH: *Only my poverty consents, not my will.*

ROM: *Then I pay your poverty, and not your will.*

APOTH: *Put this in any liquid you want and drink it all. Even if you had the strength of twenty men, it would kill you immediately.*

ROM: *There is your gold, a worse poison to men's souls, and doing more murder in this loathsome world than these poor compounds that you may not sell. I sell you poison; you have sold me none. Farewell. Buy food and get yourself fattened. Come, sweet liqueur and not poison, go with me to Juliet's grave, for there I must use you.* [Exit.]

SCENE II

Verona. Friar Laurence's Cell.

[Enter Friar John.]

JOHN: Holy Franciscan friar, brother, ho!

[Enter Friar Laurence.]

LAUR: This same should be the voice of Friar John.
    Welcome from Mantua. What says Romeo?
    Or, if his mind be writ, give me his letter.

5   JOHN: Going to find a barefoot brother out,
    One of our order, to associate me
    Here in this city visiting the sick,
    And finding him, the searchers of the town,
    Suspecting that we both were in a house
10   Where the infectious pestilence did reign,
    Seal'd up the doors, and would not let us forth,
    So that my speed to Mantua there was stay'd.

LAUR: Who bare my letter, then, to Romeo?

JOHN: I could not send it—here it is again—
15   Nor get a messenger to bring it thee,
    So fearful were they of infection.

LAUR: Unhappy fortune! By my brotherhood,
    The letter was not nice, but full of charge,
    Of dear import; and the neglecting it
20   May do much danger. Friar John, go hence,
    Get me an iron crow and bring it straight
    Unto my cell.

JOHN: Brother, I'll go and bring it thee.   *[Exit.]*

LAUR: Now, must I to the monument alone.
25   Within this three hours will fair Juliet wake.

SCENE II
Verona. Friar Laurence's Cell.

[Enter Friar John.]

JOHN: Holy Franciscan friar, brother, hello!

[Enter Friar Laurence.]

LAUR: This is certainly the voice of Friar John. Welcome from Mantua. What does Romeo say? Or, if his mind was written, give me his letter.

JOHN: I went to find a brother friar, one of our order, who assists me here in this city visiting the sick. While we two were in a house, town officials, suspecting that the house we were in was one in which the infectious plague resides, sealed up the doors and would not let us leave. As a result, my departure to Mantua was delayed.

LAUR: Who took my letter, then, to Romeo?

JOHN: I could not send it—here it is again—nor could I get a messenger to bring it to you, so fearful were they of infection.

LAUR: Unhappy fortune! By my order, the letter was not just pleasantries, but full of weighty matter of great importance, and neglecting it may bring much danger. Friar John, go and get me a crowbar and bring it immediately to my cell.

JOHN: Brother, I'll go and bring it to you.   [Exit.]

LAUR: Now, I must go to the monument alone. Within three hours, fair Juliet will waken. She will be very unhappy that Romeo has had no notice of these

She will beshrew me much that Romeo
Hath had no notice of these accidents;
But I will write again to Mantua,
And keep her at my cell till Romeo come—
30   Poor living corse, clos'd in a dead man's tomb!   *[Exit.]*

SCENE III

Verona. A Churchyard; in it, the monument of the Capulets.

[Enter Paris and his Page with flowers and a torch.]

PAR: Give me thy torch, boy. Hence, and stand aloof.
Yet put it out, for I would not be seen.
Under yond yew tree lay thee all along,
Holding thine ear close to the hollow ground.
5   So shall no foot upon the churchyard tread
(Being loose, unfirm, with digging up of graves)
But thou shalt hear it. Whistle then to me,
As signal that thou hear'st something approach.
Give me those flowers. Do as I bid thee, go.

10   PAGE: *[Aside.]* I am almost afraid to stand alone
Here in the churchyard; yet I will adventure.   *[Retires.]*

PAR: Sweet flower, with flowers thy bridal bed I strew
(O woe! thy canopy is dust and stones)
Which with sweet water nightly I will dew;
15   Or, wanting that, with tears distill'd by moans.
The obsequies that I for thee will keep
Nightly shall be to strew thy grave and weep. *[The Page whistles.]*
The boy gives warning something doth approach.
What cursed foot wanders this way to-night
20   To cross my obsequies and true love's rite?
What, with a torch? Muffle me, night, a while.   *[Retires.]*

incidents, but I will write again to Mantua and keep her in my room until Romeo comes. Poor living corpse, closed in a dead man's tomb!   [Exit.]

SCENE III

Verona. A Churchyard; in it, the monument of the Capulets.

[Enter Paris and his Page with flowers and a torch.]

PAR: *Give me your torch, boy. Leave, and stand apart. Yet put it out, for I would rather not be seen. Lie under that yew tree, holding your ear close to the hollow ground. Then, listen for any footstep in the churchyard. (Because the ground is loose and soft with digging up graves, a noise will be made.) Whistle to me then, as a signal that you hear someone approaching. Give me those flowers. Do as I bid you. Go.*

PAGE: [Aside.] *I am almost afraid to stand alone here in the churchyard; yet I will risk it.*   [Leaves.]

PAR: *Sweet flower, with these flowers I cover your bridal bed. With tears of love I will moisten it nightly, or, lacking that, with tears made pure by moans. These rites for you I will perform nightly at your grave, and I will weep.*
[The Page whistles.]
The boy gives warning of someone approaching. What cursed foot wanders tonight this way to upset my mourning and true love's rite? What, with a torch? Hide me, night, for a while.   [Leaves.]

[Enter Romeo and Balthasar with a torch, a mattock, and a crow of iron.]

Rom: Give me that mattock and the wrenching iron.
    Hold, take this letter. Early in the morning
    See thou deliver it to my lord and father.
25   Give me the light. Upon thy life I charge thee,
    Whate'er thou hearest or seest, stand all aloof
    And do not interrupt me in my course.
    Why I descend into this bed of death
    Is partly to behold my lady's face,
30   But chiefly to take thence from her dead finger
    A precious ring—a ring that I must use
    In dear employment. Therefore hence, be gone.
    But if thou, jealous, dost return to pry
    In what I further shall intend to do,
35   By heaven, I will tear thee joint by joint
    And strew this hungry churchyard with thy limbs.
    The time and my intents are savage-wild,
    More fierce and more inexorable far
    Than empty tigers or the roaring sea.

40   Bal: I will be gone, sir, and not trouble you.

Rom: So shalt thou show me friendship. Take thou that.
    Live, and be prosperous; and farewell, good fellow.

Bal: *[Aside.]* For all this same, I'll hide me hereabout.
    His looks I fear, and his intents I doubt. *[Retires.]*

45   Rom: Thou detestable maw, thou womb of death,
    Gorg'd with the dearest morsel of the earth,
    Thus I enforce thy rotten jaws to open,
    And in despite I'll cram thee with more food.
                [Romeo opens the tomb.]

Par: This is that banish'd haughty Montague
50   That murdered my love's cousin—with which grief
    It is supposed the fair creature died—
    And here is come to do some villanous shame

[Enter Romeo and Balthasar with a torch, a pick, and a crowbar.]

Rom: *Give me that pick and the crowbar. Here, take this letter. Early in the morning, see that you deliver it to my lord and father Give me the light. I order you, upon your life, whatever you hear or see, stay away and do not interrupt me. I descend into this bed of death partly to behold my lady's face but chiefly to take from her dead finger a precious ring—a ring that I must use personally. Therefore, leave; be gone. But if you are suspicious and return to pry into what I intend to do, by heaven, I will tear you limb from limb and strew this hungry churchyard with your bones. The time and my intentions are wild, more fierce and more unstoppable than hungry tigers or the roaring sea.*

Bal: *I will be gone, sir, and not trouble you.*

Rom: *Thus shall you show me friendship. Take that.* [Hands him gold.] *Live, and be prosperous; farewell, good fellow.*

Bal: [Aside.] *But all the same, I'll hide hereabouts. I fear his looks, and I doubt his intentions.* [Retires.]

Rom: *You detestable mouth, you womb of death, gorged with the dearest morsel of the earth, thus I force your rotting jaws open, and, despite everything, I'll stuff you with more food.* [Romeo opens the tomb.]

Par: *This is that banished, proud Montague who murdered my love's cousin Tybalt, whose death caused the grief from which it is thought the fair Juliet died—and here Romeo comes to do some villainous shame to the dead bodies. I will apprehend him.* [Moves forward.] *Stop your wicked work, vile*

213

To the dead bodies. I will apprehend him.
Stop thy unhallowed toil, vile Montague!
55   Can vengeance be pursu'd further than death?
Condemned villain, I do apprehend thee.
Obey, and go with me; for thou must die.

ROM: I must indeed; and therefore came I hither.
Good gentle youth, tempt not a desp'rate man.
60   Fly hence and leave me. Think upon these gone;
Let them affright thee. I beseech thee, youth,
Put not another sin upon my head
By urging me to fury. O, be gone!
By heaven, I love thee better than myself,
65   For I come hither arm'd against myself.
Stay not, be gone. Live, and hereafter say
A madman's mercy bid thee run away.

PAR: I do defy thy conjurations
And apprehend thee for a felon here.

70   ROM: Wilt thou provoke me? Then have at thee, boy! *[They fight.]*

PAGE: O Lord, they fight! I will go call the watch. *[Exit. Paris falls.]*

PAR: O, I am slain! If thou be merciful,
Open the tomb, lay me with Juliet.   *[Dies.]*

ROM: In faith, I will. Let me peruse this face.
75   Mercutio's kinsman, noble County Paris!
What said my man when my betossed soul
Did not attend him as we rode? I think
He told me Paris should have married Juliet.
Said he not so? or did I dream it so?
80   Or am I mad, hearing him talk of Juliet
To think it was so? O, give me thy hand,
One writ with me in sour misfortune's book!
I'll bury thee in a triumphant grave.
A grave? O, no, a lantern, slaughtr'd youth,
85   For here lies Juliet, and her beauty makes
This vault a feasting presence full of light.
Death, lie thou there, by a dead man interr'd.

Montague! Can vengeance be pursued further than death? Condemned villain, I stop you. Obey, and go with me, for you must die.

ROM: I must indeed, and, therefore, that is why I came here. Good gentle youth, tempt not a desperate man. Fly from here and leave me. Think upon these who are gone; let them frighten you. I beg you, youth, do not put another sin upon my head by urging me to fight. Leave! By heaven, I love you better than myself, for I come here armed against myself. Stay not, be gone. Live, and hereafter say a madman's mercy bid you run away.

PAR: I defy your solemn appeals and apprehend you for a felon here.

ROM: Will you provoke me? Then have at you, boy!   [They fight.]

PAGE: Oh, Lord, they fight! I will go call the watch.   [Exit. Paris falls.]

PAR: Oh, I am dying! If you are merciful, open the tomb, place me with Juliet. [Dies.]

ROM: In truth, I will. Let me view this face. Mercutio's kinsman, noble Count Paris! What did Balthasar say to me as we rode, when I was too preoccupied to listen to him? I think he told me Paris should have married Juliet. Did he not say it, or did I dream it? Or am I mad, hearing him talk of Juliet, to think it was so? Give me your hand, you who are written with me in the book of misfortune! I'll bury you in a magnificent grave. A grave? Oh, no, a lighted enclosure, slaughtered youth, for here also lies Juliet, and her beauty makes this vault like a banquet hall full of light. Death, lie there, by a dead man laid to rest.

[Lays him in the tomb.]

How oft when men are at the point of death
Have they been merry! which their keepers call
90   A lightning before death. O, how may I
Call this a lightning? O my love! my wife!
Death, that hath suck'd the honey of thy breath,
Hath had no power yet upon thy beauty.
Thou art not conquer'd. Beauty's ensign yet
95   Is crimson in thy lips and in thy cheeks,
And death's pale flag is not advanced there.
Tybalt, liest thou there in thy bloody sheet?
O, what more favour can I do to thee
Than with that hand that cut thy youth in twain
100   To sunder his that was thine enemy?
Forgive me, cousin. Ah, dear Juliet,
Why art thou yet so fair? Shall I believe
That unsubstantial Death is amorous,
And that the lean abhorred monster keeps
105   Thee here in dark to be his paramour?
For fear of that I still will stay with thee
And never from this palace of dim night
Depart again. Here, here will I remain
With worms that are thy chambermaids. O, here
110   Will I set up my everlasting rest
And shake the yoke of inauspicious stars
From this world-wearied flesh. Eyes, look your last!
Arms, take your last embrace! and, lips, O you
The doors of breath, seal with a righteous kiss
115   A dateless bargain to engrossing death!
Come, bitter conduct; come, unsavoury guide!
Thou desperate pilot, now at once run on
The dashing rocks thy seasick weary bark!
Here's to my love! *[Drinks.]* O true apothecary!
120   Thy drugs are quick. Thus with a kiss I die. *[Falls.]*

[Enter Friar Laurence, with lantern, crow, and spade.]

FRIAR: Saint Francis be my speed! how oft to-night
Have my old feet stumbled at graves! Who's there?

[Lays him in the tomb.]

How often when men are at the point of death do they become merry! Their keepers call it a lightening of spirit before death. How may I call this "lightening"? My love! my wife! Death, that has sucked the honey of your breath, has had no power yet upon your beauty. You are not conquered. Beauty is still crimson on your lips and in your cheeks, and death's pale flag has not advanced there. Tybalt, do you lie there in your bloody sheet? What bigger favor can I do for you than, with that hand that ended your youth take the life of your enemy? Forgive me, cousin. Ah, dear Juliet, why are you still so fair? Shall I believe that unsubstantial Death is in love and that the lean, hated monster keeps you here in the dark to be his lover? For fear of that, I still will stay with you and never depart again from this palace of dim night. Here will I remain with worms that are your maids. Oh, here will I set up my everlasting rest and shake off the harness of unfriendly stars from this world-wearied flesh. Eyes, look your last! Arms, take your last embrace! And, lips—Oh, you doors of breath—seal with a righteous kiss an endless contract to engrossing death! Come, bitter conductor of death; come, unsavory guide! You desperate pilot, now at once run your seasick, weary ship onto the dashing rocks! Here's to my love! [Drinks.] Oh, honest pharmacist! Your drugs are quick. Thus with a kiss I die.   [Falls.]

[Enter Friar Laurence, with lantern, crowbar, and spade.]

FRIAR: *Saint Francis be my aid! How often tonight have my old feet stumbled on graves! Who's there?*

Bal: Here's one, a friend, and one that knows you well.

Friar: Bliss be upon you! Tell me, good my friend,
125   What torch is yond that vainly lends his light
To grubs and eyeless skulls? As I discern,
It burneth in the Capels' monument.

Bal: It doth so, holy sir; and there's my master,
One that you love.

130   Friar: Who is it?

Bal: Romeo.

Friar: How long hath he been there?

Bal: Full half an hour.

Friar: Go with me to the vault.

135   Bal: I dare not, sir.
My master knows not but I am gone hence,
And fearfully did menace me with death
If I did stay to look on his intents.

Friar: Stay then; I'll go alone. Fear comes upon me.
140   O, much I fear some ill unlucky thing.

Bal: As I did sleep under this yew tree here,
I dreamt my master and another fought,
And that my master slew him.

Friar: Romeo!
145   Alack, alack, what blood is this which stains
The stony entrance of this sepulchre?
What mean these masterless and gory swords
To lie discolour'd by this place of peace?   *[Enters the tomb.]*
Romeo! O, pale! Who else? What, Paris too?
150   And steep'd in blood? Ah, what an unkind hour
Is guilty of this lamentable chance! The lady stirs.   *[Juliet rises.]*

218

BAL: Here's one who is a friend and one that knows you well.

FRIAR: Happiness be upon you! Tell me, my good friend, what torch is there that vainly lends his light to grubs and eyeless skulls? As I see it, it burns in the Capulets' monument.

BAL: It does so, holy sir, and there's my master, one whom you love.

FRIAR: Who is it?

BAL: Romeo.

FRIAR: How long has he been there?

BAL: Fully half an hour.

FRIAR: Go with me to the vault.

BAL: I dare not, sir. My master does not know that I am not gone, and he fearfully threatened me with death if I did stay to look on his plans.

FRIAR: Stay then; I'll go alone. Fear comes upon me. Oh, much do I fear that some ill, unlucky thing has happened.

BAL: As I did sleep under this yew tree here, I dreamed that my master and another fought and that my master slew him.

FRIAR: Romeo! Alas, alas, whose blood is this that stains the stony entrance of this tomb? What do these masterless and gory swords mean lying bloody near this place of peace? [Enters the tomb.] Romeo! Oh, so pale! Who else? What, Paris too? And covered in blood? Ah, what an unkind hour is guilty of this lamentable event! The lady stirs. [Juliet rises.]

JUL: O comfortable friar! where is my lord?
    I do remember well where I should be,
    And there I am. Where is my Romeo?

155 FRIAR: I hear some noise. Lady, come from that nest
    Of death, contagion, and unnatural sleep.
    A greater power than we can contradict
    Hath thwarted our intents. Come, come away.
    Thy husband in thy bosom there lies dead;
160   And Paris too. Come, I'll dispose of thee
    Among a sisterhood of holy nuns.
    Stay not to question, for the watch is coming.
    Come, go, good Juliet. I dare no longer stay.

JUL: Go, get thee hence, for I will not away.   *[Exit Friar.]*
165   What's here? A cup, clos'd in my true love's hand?
    Poison, I see, hath been his timeless end.
    O churl! drunk all, and left no friendly drop
    To help me after? I will kiss thy lips.
    Haply some poison yet doth hang on them
170   To make me die with a restorative. *[Kisses him.]*
    Thy lips are warm!

CHIEF WATCH: *[Within.]* Lead, boy. Which way?

JUL: Yea, noise? Then I'll be brief. O happy dagger!
      [Snatches Romeo's dagger.]
    This is thy sheath; there rust, and let me die.
      [She stabs herself and falls on Romeo's body.]

[Enter Paris's Boy and Watch.]

175 BOY: This is the place. There, where the torch doth burn.

CHIEF WATCH: The ground is bloody. Search about the churchyard.
    Go, some of you; who e'er you find attach.
               [Exeunt some of the Watch.]
    Pitiful sight! here lies the County slain;
    And Juliet bleeding, warm, and newly dead,
180   Who here hath lain this two days buried.

JUL: *Oh, friendly friar! Where is my lord? I do remember well where I should be, and here I am. Where is my Romeo?*

FRIAR: *I hear some noise. Lady, come from this nest of death, contagion, and unnatural sleep. A greater power than we can oppose has thwarted our intentions. Come, come away. The husband of your heart lies dead, and Paris too. Come, I'll move you to a sisterhood of holy nuns. Do not stay to question this, for the watchmen are coming. Come, go, good Juliet. I dare stay no longer.*

JUL: *Go, get away; for I will not leave.* [Exit Friar.]
What's here? A cup, closed in my true love's hand? Poison, I see, has been his timeless end. Oh, fool! You drank all, and left no friendly drop to help me leave here? I will kiss your lips. Happily some poison does yet hang on them to make me die with a drink which will restore me to you. [Kisses him.] *Your lips are warm!*

CHIEF WATCH: [Within.] *Lead, boy. Which way?*

JUL: *What, a noise? Then I'll be brief. Oh, happy dagger!*
[Snatches Romeo's dagger.]
This is your sheath; rust there, and let me die.
[She stabs herself and falls on Romeo's body.]

[Enter Paris' Boy and Watchmen.]

BOY: *This is the place. There—where the torch burns.*

CHIEF WATCH: *The ground is bloody. Search about the churchyard. Go, some of you; arrest whomever you find.* [Exit some of the Watch.]
Pitiful sight! Here lies Paris slain and Juliet bleeding, warm, and newly dead, who has lain here these two days already buried. Go, tell the Prince; run to the Capulets; raise up the Montagues; some others search the grounds.
[Exit others of the Watch.]

Go, tell the Prince; run to the Capulets;
Raise up the Montagues; some others search.
[Exeunt others of the Watch.]
We see the ground whereon these woes do lie,
But the true ground of all these piteous woes
185   We cannot without circumstance descry.

[Enter some of the Watch, with Romeo's Man Balthasar.]

2. WATCH: Here's Romeo's man. We found him in the churchyard.

CHIEF WATCH: Hold him in safety till the Prince come hither.

[Enter Friar Laurence and another Watchman.]

3. WATCH: Here is a friar that trembles, sighs, and weeps.
We took this mattock and this spade from him
190   As he was coming from this churchyard side.

CHIEF WATCH: A great suspicion! Stay the friar too.

[Enter the Prince and Attendants.]

PRINCE: What misadventure is so early up,
That calls our person from our morning rest?

[Enter Capulet, Lady Capulet, and others.]

CAP: What should it be, that they so shriek abroad?

195   LADY CAPULET: The people in the street cry 'Romeo,'
Some 'Juliet,' and some 'Paris'; and all run,
With open outcry, toward our monument.

PRINCE: What fear is this which startles in our ears?

CHIEF WATCH: Sovereign, here lies the County Paris slain;
200   And Romeo dead; and Juliet, dead before,
Warm and new kill'd.

We see the ground where these woes lie, but the true cause of all these piteous woes we cannot figure out without details.

[Enter some of the Watch, with Romeo's Man, Balthasar.]

2. WATCH: *Here's Romeo's man. We found him in the churchyard.*

CHIEF WATCH: *Hold him in safety till the Prince comes here.*

[Enter Friar Laurence and another Watchman.]

3. WATCH: *Here is a friar who trembles, sighs, and weeps. We took this pick and this shovel from him as he was coming from this side of the churchyard.*

CHIEF WATCH: *It's very suspicious! Seize the friar, too.*

[Enter the Prince and Attendants.]

PRINCE: *What is the problem that so early calls me from my morning rest?*

[Enter Capulet, Lady Capulet ,and others.]

CAP: *What is it that the crowd so shrieks about?*

LADY CAPULET: *The people in the street cry "Romeo," some "Juliet," and some "Paris," and they all run with loud screaming toward our tomb.*

PRINCE: *What fear is this which rises to our ears?*

CHIEF WATCH: *Sovereign, here lies the County Paris slain, and Romeo dead, and Juliet, who was dead before, warm and newly killed.*

PRINCE: Search, seek, and know how this foul murder comes.

CHIEF WATCH: Here is a friar, and slaughter'd Romeo's man,
    With instruments upon them fit to open
205   These dead men's tombs.

CAP: O heavens! O wife, look how our daughter bleeds!
    This dagger hath mista'en, for, lo, his house
    Is empty on the back of Montague,
    And it missheathed in my daughter's bosom!

210   LADY CAPULET: O me! this sight of death is as a bell
    That warns my old age to a sepulchre.

[Enter Montague and others.]

PRINCE: Come, Montague; for thou art early up
    To see thy son and heir more early down.

MON: Alas, my liege, my wife is dead to-night!
215   Grief of my son's exile hath stopp'd her breath.
    What further woe conspires against mine age?

PRINCE: Look, and thou shalt see.

MON: O thou untaught! what manners is in this,
    To press before thy father to a grave?

220   PRINCE: Seal up the mouth of outrage for a while,
    Till we can clear these ambiguities
    And know their spring, their head, their true descent;
    And then will I be general of your woes
    And lead you even to death. Meantime forbear,
225   And let mischance be slave to patience.
    Bring forth the parties of suspicion.

FRIAR: I am the greatest, able to do least,
    Yet most suspected, as the time and place
    Doth make against me, of this direful murder;
230   And here I stand, both to impeach and purge
    Myself condemned and myself excus'd.

PRINCE: *Search, seek, and know how this foul murder came about.*

CHIEF WATCH: *Here is a friar, and Romeo's man, with tools on them fit to open these dead men's tombs.*

CAP: *Oh, heavens! Oh, wife, look how our daughter bleeds! This dagger has plunged into the wrong spot. Romeo's scabbard lies empty on his back, and the dagger is misplaced in my daughter's chest!*

LADY CAPULET: *Oh, me! This sight of death is as a bell that warns my old age of a future tomb.*

[Enter Montague and others.]

PRINCE: [bitterly] *Come, Montague for you are up early to see your son and heir buried early.*

MON: *Alas, my lord, my wife is dead tonight! Grief of my son's exile has stopped her breath. What further woe conspires against my age?*

PRINCE: *Look, and you shall see.*

MON: *Romeo, you ignorant boy! What manners are these, to push ahead of your father towards a grave?*

PRINCE: *Restrain yourself until we can clear up these puzzles and know their source, their head and, their true beginning; then I will take charge of your woes and lead you even to death. In the meantime wait, and let this calamity be ruled by patience. Bring forth the parties under suspicion.*

FRIAR: *According to this time and place I am the greatest suspect in this terrible crime, but while I stand here guilty of the crime, I am guiltless of any wrong intentions.*

PRINCE: Then say at once what thou dost know in this.

FRIAR: I will be brief, for my short date of breath
   Is not so long as is a tedious tale.
235 Romeo, there dead, was husband to that Juliet;
   And she, there dead, that Romeo's faithful wife.
   I married them; and their stol'n marriage day
   Was Tybalt's doomsday, whose untimely death
   Banish'd the new-made bridegroom from this city;
240 For whom, and not for Tybalt, Juliet pin'd.
   You, to remove that siege of grief from her,
   Betroth'd and would have married her perforce
   To County Paris. Then comes she to me
   And with wild looks bid me devise some mean
245 To rid her from this second marriage,
   Or in my cell there would she kill herself.
   Then gave I her (so tutored by my art)
   A sleeping potion; which so took effect
   As I intended, for it wrought on her
250 The form of death. Meantime I writ to Romeo
   That he should hither come as this dire night
   To help to take her from her borrowed grave,
   Being the time the potion's force should cease.
   But he which bore my letter, Friar John,
255 Was stay'd by accident, and yesternight
   Return'd my letter back. Then all alone
   At the prefixed hour of her waking
   Came I to take her from her kindred's vault;
   Meaning to keep her closely at my cell
260 Till I conveniently could send to Romeo.
   But when I came, some minute ere the time
   Of her awaking, here untimely lay
   The noble Paris and true Romeo dead.
   She wakes; and I entreated her come forth
265 And bear this work of heaven with patience;
   But then a noise did scare me from the tomb,
   And she, too desperate, would not go with me,
   But, as it seems, did violence on herself.
   All this I know, and to the marriage
270 Her Nurse is privy; and if aught in this

PRINCE: *Then say at once what you know about this.*

FRIAR: *I will be brief, for my short life is not as long as this complicated tale. Romeo, there dead, was husband to that Juliet. She, there dead, was Romeo's faithful wife. I married them, and their stolen marriage day was Tybalt's doomsday, whose untimely death caused Romeo to be banished from this city. It was for Romeo, not for Tybalt, that Juliet wept. To remove that grief from her, Lord Capulet betrothed her and would have married her to County Paris. Then she came to me and with wild looks bid me to devise some means to rid her of this second marriage, or in my cell she would kill herself. I then gave her a sleeping potion which took effect exactly as I intended, for it gave her the appearance of death. In the meantime, I wrote to Romeo that he should come here this night to take Juliet from her borrowed grave, since by then the potion's force should stop. But he who bore my letter, Friar John, was stopped by accident and last evening returned my letter. Since Juliet would be all alone at the predicted hour of her waking, I came to take her from her family's vault. I intended to keep her close by my cell until I could conveniently send for Romeo. But when I got here some minutes before the time of her awaking, I found the noble Paris and Romeo both dead. When she woke, I begged her to bear her sorrow with patience, but then a noise scared me from the tomb. She would not go with me but, as it looks, did this violence on herself. All this I know, and of the marriage her Nurse also knows. If any of this that went wrong is my fault, let my old life be sacrificed, some hour before my time, under the penalty of the severest law.*

Miscarried by my fault, let my old life
Be sacrific'd, some hour before his time,
Unto the rigour of severest law.

PRINCE: We still have known thee for a holy man.
275   Where's Romeo's man? What can he say in this?

BAL: I brought my master news of Juliet's death;
        And then in post he came from Mantua
        To this same place, to this same monument.
        This letter he early bid me give his father,
280   And threat'ned me with death, going in the vault,
        If I departed not and left him there.

PRINCE: Give me the letter. I will look on it.
        Where is the County's page that rais'd the watch?
        Sirrah, what made your master in this place?

285   BOY: He came with flowers to strew his lady's grave;
        And bid me stand aloof, and so I did.
        Anon comes one with light to ope the tomb;
        And by-and-by my master drew on him;
        And then I ran away to call the watch.

290   PRINCE: This letter doth make good the friar's words,
        Their course of love, the tidings of her death;
        And here he writes that he did buy a poison
        Of a poor 'pothecary, and therewithal
        Came to this vault to die, and lie with Juliet.
295   Where be these enemies? Capulet, Montage,
        See what a scourge is laid upon your hate,
        That heaven finds means to kill your joys with love!
        And I, for winking at you, discords too,
        Have lost a brace of kinsmen. All are punish'd.

300   CAP: O brother Montague, give me thy hand.
        This is my daughter's jointure, for no more
        Can I demand.

PRINCE: We have known you for a holy man. Where's Romeo's man? What can he say about this?

BAL: I brought my master news of Juliet's death, and then he came from Mantua in haste to this place, to this same monument. This letter he asked me to give to his father. He threatened me with death, while going in the vault, if I did not depart and leave him there.

PRINCE: Give me the letter. I will look at it. Where is Paris' man who woke the watch? Sir, what made your master come to this place?

BOY: He came with flowers to throw on his lady's grave and bid me stand away, and so I did. Soon someone comes with a light to open the tomb, and soon after my master drew his sword on him, and then I ran away to call the Watch.

PRINCE: This letter does confirm the friar's words, their course of love, and the news of her death. Here he writes that he did buy some poison from a poor pharmacist and came with it to this vault to die and to lie with Juliet. Where are these enemies? Capulet! Montague! See what a plague is laid upon your hate, that heaven found ways to kill your offspring with love! And I, for being lenient with you and your fights, have lost a pair of relatives. All are punished.

CAP: Oh, brother Montague, give me your handshake. This is my daughter's dowry; of nothing more will I demand.

MON: But I can give thee more;
    For I will raise her statue in pure gold,
305   That whiles Verona by that name is known,
    There shall no figure at such rate be set
    As that of true and faithful Juliet.

CAP: As rich shall Romeo's by his lady's lie—
    Poor sacrifices of our enmity!

310   PRINCE: A glooming peace this morning with it brings.
    The sun for sorrow will not show his head.
    Go hence, to have more talk of these sad things;
    Some shall be pardon'd, and some punished;
    For never was a story of more woe
315   Than this of Juliet and her Romeo.

[Exeunt omnes.]

MON: But I can give you more, for I will raise her statue in pure gold. While Verona is known by that name, there shall never be a statue set which is more valuable than that of true and faithful Juliet.

CAP: An equally rich statue of Romeo will lie by his lady—poor victims of our hatred!

PRINCE: This morning brings a gloomy peace. In sorrow, the sun will not show his head. Leave here, and talk more about these sad things; some shall be pardoned, and some punished. For never was there a story of more woe than this of Juliet and her Romeo.

[All Exit.]

Study Guide

1. Where is this play set?

2. What problem exists in this city?

3. What does the term "star-crossed lovers" suggest?

Act I, Scene 1 - A Street in Verona

1. Sampson and Gregory, servants to the Capulets, are bragging, vulgar-mouthed men who engage in word games. What bawdy comment does Sampson make?

2. What is there about the talk and actual actions of Gregory and Sampson that suggests that they are not as brave and tough as they pretend? Give an example of their actions that contradicts their talk.

3. Who is Benvolio and what does he attempt to do?

4. How does Tybalt, a Capulet, misinterpret Benvolio's action? What does he say to him?

5. Why is Tybalt considered hot-tempered?

6. What remark of Lady Capulet says something about Lord Capulet's age and condition?

7. What do you suppose prompts Lady Montague to hold her husband back from the fight?

8. The Prince appears, and he is angry. Why is he angry and what is the promise (or threat) he makes?

9. Lady Montague, glad that Romeo missed the fight, asks Benvolio if he has seen Romeo. What is Benvolio's response?

10. At this point, what is Lady Montague worried about?

11. Romeo enters and tells Benvolio the problem. What is Romeo's problem?

12. What is Benvolio's response?

13. Although both are saddened by unaccepted love, what joke are they able to make?

14. What practical advice does Benvolio give Romeo?

Act I, Scene 2 - Lord Capulet's House

1. After some small talk, Paris gets to the point of his visit. What is it that he asks of Capulet?

2. What is Capulet's response?

3. Paris says that girls younger than Juliet have been married. What is Capulet's response to this?

4. What suggestion and invitation does Capulet make to Paris?

5. Romeo, lamenting over Rosaline, is approached by the illiterate servingman. In reading a guest list, Romeo finds that Rosaline, his love, is going to attend the Capulet party. What suggestion does Benvolio make?

Act I, Scene 3 - Capulet's House

1. The Nurse quotes the bawdy remark that her husband has made to the young Juliet and then likes it so much that she repeats it. What do the Nurse's indecent remarks in front of the family indicate about her relationship with the Capulets?

2. What does Juliet's mother tell Juliet?

3. What is Juliet's response?

Act I, Scene 4 - A Street by Capulet's House

1. Why does Romeo say he will not be able to dance?

2. How do these Montagues expect to be able to enter a Capulet house?

3. Romeo seems to believe that our dreams have something to do with our lives; perhaps, dreams act as an omen. What is Mercutio's opinion of dreams?

4. How does Mercutio end this conversation?

5. What is Romeo's misgiving, and what does the line "some consequence yet hanging in the stars" have to do with his feeling of dread?

Act I, Scene 5 - Capulet's House

1. Lord Capulet and a relative stand, unmasked, on one side of the room. Romeo, masked, standing on the other side, asks a serving-man who a certain pretty girl is. How does Romeo describe the girl and what does he conclude?

2. What is hot-tempered Tybalt's reaction when he hears Romeo's voice?

3. What does Lord Capulet say to Tybalt?

4. Tybalt obeys his uncle, but what does he vow?

5. Romeo, going up to Juliet, begins a conversation and ends up kissing her twice before the Nurse comes and tells Juliet that her mother wants her. Romeo and his friends leave. How do we know that Juliet feels as strongly about Romeo as he does about her?

Act II - Chorus

1. The chorus comments on the action of the play. Put in your own words the meaning of the first four lines.

2. What problem of the lovers does the chorus allude to?

3. What is the suggested solution to their problem?

Act II, Scene 1 - Outside of Capulet's House

1. Romeo slips away from his friends and the practical, vulgar Mercutio makes some indecent comments about Rosaline. What truth does the audience know?

Act II, Scene 2 - Capulet's Garden Outside Juliet's Window

1. This is one of the most famous of Shakespeare's soliloquies. What is Romeo doing?

2. What is Juliet saying?

3. Why, at this point, is Juliet suddenly startled?

4. As Juliet points out, Romeo is risking death by being there. What is his response?

5. Since Romeo has overheard her private thoughts, what is Juliet's greatest concern?

6. When Romeo swears by the moon, what does Juliet tell him?

7. After an exchange of vows, the Nurse calls and Juliet must leave. What is Romeo's feeling as he stands there?

8. Juliet then reappears. What does she tell Romeo?

9. What decision does Romeo make?

Act II, Scene 3 - Outside the Friar's Monastery

1. The Friar, guessing that Romeo is out early because he was up all night, assumes that Romeo has been with Rosaline. When Romeo informs him that it is not Rosaline he wishes to marry but somebody else, what is the Friar's reaction?

2. How is the Friar making fun of Romeo?

3. Why does the Friar agree to help Romeo and Juliet get married?

Act II, Scene 4 - A Street Near the Montague House

1. As Romeo enters, Mercutio and Benvolio are discussing Romeo's longing for Rosaline and Tybalt's challenge to Romeo. What change in Romeo's behavior does Mercutio comment on?

2. After Benvolio and Mercutio leave, the Nurse asks, in effect, about the wise guy. What is Romeo's answer?

3. The Nurse, angry and upset with Mercutio and with Peter who just stood there while she was being insulted, expresses what doubts about Romeo?

4. What is the message that Romeo gives the Nurse to give to Juliet?

5. What is it that Romeo's man is to bring to the Nurse for Juliet?

Act II, Scene 5 - Juliet's House

1. As Juliet waits for the Nurse to return, what is her mood?

2. How does the Nurse tease Juliet?

3. Finally, what does the Nurse tell Juliet?

4. The Nurse informs Juliet that she is off to fetch the rope ladder. What is this rope ladder to be used for?

Act II, Scene 6 - Friar Lawrence's Cell in the Monastery

1. The Friar seems to have some doubts about the wisdom of what he is about to do. Romeo responds that after he is married to Juliet, death can do what it dares to him. What reservations does the Friar express?

2. Juliet enters. What is the mood that Romeo expresses, and the mood that Juliet expresses?

3. What follows after they exit from the stage?

Act III, Scene 1 - A Street in Verona

1. How does Benvolio show himself to be a reasoning man?

2. What is Mercutio's response?

3. What is Romeo's response to Tybalt's challenge and to Tybalt's insult? (Tybalt calls Romeo a villain.)

4. In what way is Romeo responsible for Mercutio being stabbed?

5. In what way is Mercutio's comment about his wound sarcastic?

6. What is Romeo's reaction to Mercutio's death?

7. What does Lady Capulet request of the Prince?

8. What is the Prince's decision?

Act III, Scene 2 - Capulet House

1. As Juliet impatiently waits for night and Romeo's visit, the Nurse arrives with news. What is the Nurse's news and in what manner does she present it?

2. Juliet's first reaction is to call Romeo vile names for having killed Tybalt, but what is her second reaction?

3. Why does the Nurse, who was obviously fond of Tybalt, volunteer to go and get Romeo?

4. Where is Romeo hiding, what seems to be Juliet's plan, and why does she give the Nurse a ring?

Act III, Scene 3 - Friar Lawrence's Cell

1. How does Romeo react to the news that he has been banished?

2. Why can't the Friar, according to Romeo, truly understand Romeo's feelings about Juliet and his banishment?

3. The Nurse arrives and informs the Friar and Romeo that Juliet, too, is crying, just as Romeo is. Hearing of Juliet's unhappiness and the hatred he supposes she feels toward him, he draws his knife to kill himself. What does the Friar accuse him of?

4. For what things does the Friar say Romeo should be happy?

Act III, Scene 4 - Capulet's House

1. In the conversation between Lord Capulet, his wife, and Paris, we learn that they have not yet spoken to Juliet about marrying Paris. What do they think is Juliet's present cause of grief?

2. What decision does Lord Capulet make, and why do you suppose he makes this decision?

Act III, Scene 5 - Romeo and Juliet at Juliet's Window as Dawn is Breaking

1. What is going on in the interchange between Romeo and Juliet at the opening of this scene?

2. Lady Capulet enters and, seeing Juliet weeping at Romeo's departure, believes her daughter is weeping for Tybalt. Lady Capulet then vents her own anger at Romeo and discloses her plan to have him found and poisoned. Why does Juliet appear to speak ill of Romeo?

3. What news does Juliet's mother bring?

4. What is Juliet's response to her mother?

5. Why does Lord Capulet get angry when he hears of Juliet's desire not to marry?

6. When the Nurse tries to speak up for Juliet, what is she told?

7. If forced to marry, what does Juliet threaten?

8. What is her mother's response?

9 What is the Nurse's advice, and how could she give that advice knowing how Juliet feels?

10. What is Juliet's decision regarding the Nurse?

11. Juliet tells the Nurse she is going to Friar Lawrence to confess her sins. Why is she really going there?

Act IV, Scene 1 - Friar Lawrence's Cell

1. What does Juliet tell the Friar?

2. What plan does the Friar set out?

Act IV, Scene 2 - Capulet's House

1. Why is Lord Capulet happy?

Act IV, Scene 3 - Capulet's House, Juliet's Room

1. If the potion does not work, what is Juliet's plan?

2. Juliet is a little fearful and a little suspicious. What suspicion about the Friar does she voice?

Act IV, Scene 4 - Capulet House, the Next Morning

1. In the interchange between the Nurse, Lord Capulet, and his wife, what does his wife accuse Capulet of?

2. What does all the action in the house indicate?

Act IV, Scene 5 - Juliet's Bedroom

1. How do the Capulets react to the news of Juliet's death?

2. Does their grief seem sincere?

3. How does the Friar try to comfort them?

4. The next bit between Peter and the musicians seems to be for "comic relief." How do you suppose the scene is supposed to function in the play?

Act V, Scene 1 - A Street in Mantua

1. The Friar was supposed to send a messenger to Romeo informing him of the plan and Juliet's fake death. Who arrives in Mantua instead, and what news does he give Romeo?

2. Although it is illegal to sell poisons in Mantua, how is Romeo able to purchase some?

Act V, Scene 2 - Friar Lawrence's Cell

1. Why is Friar John not able to go to Mantua and deliver Friar Lawrence's message to Romeo?

2. What revision does Friar Lawrence make in his plan?

Act V, Scene 3 - Verona. A Churchyard

1. What is Paris doing at the crypt?

2. What does Romeo give to Balthasar, and what does he tell him to do? Why doesn't Balthasar do it?

3. Why do Paris and Romeo fight, since Romeo really has no wish to fight anyone?

4. Although Romeo has just fatally wounded Paris, what act of compassion does he perform for Paris?

6. Who or what does the Friar say "thwarted" all their plans?

7. When Juliet refuses to leave, what does the Friar do?

8. What does Juliet do?

9. What has happened to Romeo's mother?

10. The concluding lines state a major theme in this play. State what
    these lines mean and how they reflect a theme in this play.